Routledge Revivals

China in the Family of Nations

This title, first published in 1923, aimed to provide a brief survey of the historical setting necessary for an understanding of China's relations with the West. The book explained and estimated the various forces that were working in China at the beginning of the twentieth century that were producing changes in the political, social, industrial and intellectual spheres. This book will be of interest to students of history and Asian Studies.

China in the
Family of Nations

Henry T. Hodgkin

First published in 1923
by George Allen & Unwin

This edition first published in 2015 by Routledge
2 Park Square, Milton Park, Abingdon, Oxon, OX14 4RN
and by Routledge
711 Third Avenue, New York, NY 10017

Routledge is an imprint of the Taylor & Francis Group, an informa business

© 1923 Henry T. Hodgkin

All rights reserved. No part of this book may be reprinted or reproduced or utilised in any form or by any electronic, mechanical, or other means, now known or hereafter invented, including photocopying and recording, or in any information storage or retrieval system, without permission in writing from the publishers.

Publisher's Note
The publisher has gone to great lengths to ensure the quality of this reprint but points out that some imperfections in the original copies may be apparent.

Disclaimer
The publisher has made every effort to trace copyright holders and welcomes correspondence from those they have been unable to contact.

A Library of Congress record exists under LC control number: 23011909

ISBN 13: 978-1-138-92012-5 (hbk)
ISBN 13: 978-1-315-68733-9 (ebk)
ISBN 13: 978-1-138-92014-9 (pbk)

CHINA IN THE FAMILY OF NATIONS

BY

HENRY T. HODGKIN, M.A., M.B.
Secretary of the National Christian Council of China

UNDER HEAVEN THERE IS BUT ONE FAMILY

LONDON : GEORGE ALLEN & UNWIN LTD.
RUSKIN HOUSE, 40 MUSEUM STREET, W.C. 1

First published in 1923

(All rights reserved)

Printed in Great Britain by
UNWIN BROTHERS, LIMITED, THE GRESHAM PRESS, LONDON AND WOKING

TO THE CHINESE STUDENTS WHO HAVE STUDIED

OR ARE NOW STUDYING IN BRITAIN

I DEDICATE THIS BOOK

IN THE HOPE THAT IT MAY HELP

MY FELLOW-COUNTRYMEN TO UNDERSTAND

SOME OF THEIR FEELINGS AND ASPIRATIONS

AND SO TO

SEEK FOR A NATIONAL POLICY TOWARDS

CHINA, ANIMATED BY RESPECT,

THE SPIRIT OF FAIR PLAY AND INTELLIGENT SYMPATHY.

PREFACE

THE problem of China is rightly claiming far more attention from the English-speaking public to-day than was the case five-and-twenty years ago. During that time I have been fairly continuously a student of China and the Chinese, partly from a distance, but also during a residence of several years in the far-western province of Szechwan, and especially recently in extensive travel for nearly two years in China, Japan and Korea.

In the following pages I have tried to do three things : First, to give a brief survey of the historical setting necessary for an understanding of China's present relations with the West ; second, to explain and estimate the various forces now working in China, producing changes in the political, social, industrial and intellectual spheres ; and, third, to supply a point of view which may help the reader in further study or as he watches the unfolding drama.

While I cannot escape the charge of looking at these many questions with strong pro-Chinese sympathies, I claim to speak as one who has brought to his task a critical judgment as well as a sincere respect for the subjects of my study. China has too often been treated as a land of mystery which intrigues and eludes the observer. I seek to emphasize rather the far more significant fact of our kinship, our common human nature. In the Chinese I find people who are quick to make contacts, appreciative of kindness and sympathy, easy in their manners, adaptable, honourable, full of gratitude and loyalty. Among them I count some of my closest friends, and I do not feel any racial barriers in our intercourse.

Yet China holds, in very truth, a deep mystery. The wonder of China is that of a great nation preserving its unique character and its own social structure for scores of generations, and to-day entering into the broad stream of the world's life to give and to receive at a thousand points of contact. What new essence is to emerge from the mingling of these different elements ? Whither are we to be borne as the river swells and overflows its banks ? In the answer to such questions lies the deeper mystery of China.

No writer on China dare claim to be a prophet. All one can do is to state the facts, seeking to set them in true proportion and to estimate something of their meaning. These, broadly speaking, are the facts out of which the future must be shaped. We who read and write are factors of no small import in the shaping of the future, as I hope this volume may make clear.

China is no dead or dying nation. Arrested her development may have been for some centuries, but I prefer to think of these centuries as the resting stage during which she has been gathering strength for new and greater tasks. Is Europe determined to destroy herself by continued wars and enmities ? China, perchance, is yet to arise, not as the menace we have dreaded, but as the prophet of peace and reasonableness, whose voice will be heard across the stormy waters summoning us to a kindlier and saner life.

Whether this be a vain dream or a realizable possibility depends in no small measure upon just such

PREFACE

persons as the readers of this volume, persons seriously interested in the progress of humanity and alive to the possibilities of the Far East. But it is not so much our deliberate ill-will which is to be feared as a means of turning China from the paths of peace. It is our uninformed and nerveless goodwill which may yet spoil the fair picture ; it is the greed of gain which blinds men to the claims of righteousness, it is the indifference born of contempt or even of mere ignorance. To the removal of these things I would direct my own energy, and in that task I look for many a colleague among the readers of this volume.

My thanks are due to the authorities at the Selly Oak Colleges for inviting me to give the lectures which form the basis of the following chapters, to my friends Dr. T. T. Lew and Dr. Phillippe de Vargas, of Peking, for suggestions and information embodied in the chapter on the New Thought Movement, and to various friends and writers, too numerous to mention, whose ideas have been freely used to correct or modify my own experience and impressions. I cannot close this preface without a word of deepest satisfaction in the announcement just made that Britain will hand back to China the remainder of the Boxer indemnity. No act could augur better for the future relations of the two countries.

HENRY T. HODGKIN.

New Year's Day, 1923.

CONTENTS

		PAGE
PREFACE		9

CHAPTER
I.	WHY DISCUSS CHINA?	15
II.	THE TREASURES OF THE PAST	23
III.	EARLY INTERNATIONAL CONNECTIONS (BEFORE 1840)	37
IV.	COMING INTO THE FAMILY (1840–1911)	56
V.	THE REPUBLIC OF CHINA	78
VI.	JAPAN IN CHINA	100
VII.	JAPAN IN CHINA (*continued*)	118
VIII.	CHINA, EUROPE AND AMERICA	143
IX.	THE INDUSTRIALIZATION OF CHINA	171
X.	THE NEW THOUGHT MOVEMENT	197
XI.	CHINA'S GIFT TO THE WORLD	225
	BIBLIOGRAPHY	253
	INDEX	257

CHINA IN THE FAMILY OF NATIONS

CHAPTER I

WHY DISCUSS CHINA ?

It is still unfortunately true that very many people simply regard China as irrelevant. Discussion of international questions may be carried on for hours without a mention of China. Economic problems are "thrashed out" as if there were no such country. China is an interesting side-issue, a subject for detached speculation much as we discuss the possible inhabitants of Mars. This attitude of mind is found not only among the ignorant and parochially-minded, but also among persons of wide culture and interests. It may be explained in part by the remoteness of China, in part by her policy, through many generations, of "splendid isolation," and in part by the difficulty of understanding her which is commonly felt by Western minds. Whatever the explanation the fact is regrettable. I hope it may be possible in this volume so to put China and her problems into the centre of the picture, not only to cure all my readers of this particular malady, but even to make them physicians for others whose eyesight is similarly affected.

China and the Chinese are not simply a topic

of passing, if considerable, interest. Every now and again something happens which forces even the newspaper-reader to think about China. For a few days or weeks he realizes that there are infinite possibilities of good or ill in that ancient land. Then the crisis passes, and he turns his attention to a boxing match or a divorce case. But China and her people demand not a moment's passing attention but close and continuous study. Such study makes some demands upon most of us whose minds are more accustomed to think in terms of our own civilization and problems. Happily, we now have a considerable and varied literature in English which deals with China. It is not very difficult to get the main facts. What is more difficult is to enter upon the problem with real understanding. In what I have to say I shall not attempt to recount all the facts that are needed to form an estimate of China's position in the family of nations. My aim is rather to give a point of view, a clue whereby these facts may be understood and put into their right place. In doing this I frankly confess myself to be pro-Chinese in sympathy, to be a believer in China's future, and a lover of her people. At the same time I hope I may be able to present the situation in a fair way, and to avoid the danger of misrepresenting either those who differ from me, or those nations which in the past have caused China to suffer.

Let us begin by considering the factors in the situation which make the problems of China so important and relevant for Western students. It is perhaps scarcely necessary to insist upon the mere question of the size of China's population, for bulk alone does not give significance to a people any more than to an individual. China has for many centuries contained a very large population, although, if we

WHY DISCUSS CHINA ?

could trust the various estimates that have been made, it has undergone amazing fluctuations. There has been as much as 60,000,000 difference in two estimates made in the same year, and the population is supposed to have multiplied by nearly four in a quarter of a century and to have decreased from 60 to 21 millions in about eighty years (from 1580–1662)! I think it fair to assume that there are now not fewer than 350,000,000 people living in China proper, but I doubt if an accurate census would reveal a figure much in excess of that. It is also probable that the rate of increase is very considerable. I was given about 400,000 a year as the figures of Japanese increase and, if China be six or seven times more populous, we may assume not less than 2,000,000 a year as her rate of growth, allowing for a much larger death rate, which is very likely the case.

The first significant thing about these figures is the necessity of emigration imposed upon the Chinese people, and the nature of the people thus compelled. No doubt China, as all other countries, can be so developed as to sustain a much larger population if her industries are multiplied and her resources tapped, her internal organization perfected, her irrigation system improved and the area of arable land increased. But these improvements are not at present keeping pace with the growth of population, with the result that a constant stream of Chinese makes its way into the Straits Settlements, Borneo, Sumatra, the Philippines, and other neighbouring lands and islands. Chinese are knocking at the doors of Canada, America, Australia, and other countries where the white population predominates, and only the fact of China's political and military impotence prevents this persistent knocking from raising serious international problems.

Already the development of neighbouring countries

has been and is being profoundly influenced by Chinese colonization. Twenty years ago I was told that the leading doctor and the leading lawyer in Singapore were Chinese by race though British by nationality. Chinese are showing their ability to compete with Westerners in every walk of life. They have a genius for colonization second only, even if second, to that of the British, and far in advance of the Japanese or any other Eastern race. They can "make do" with the most unlikely things, and get along on what would be starvation wages to almost any other people. In a recent Japanese investigation into conditions in Moukden it was found that two neighbouring shops, owned by a Japanese and a Chinese respectively, were selling the same article at very different prices. The former seemed to be making no more than a fair profit, but his neighbour was so greatly underselling him that scarcely any custom came his way. Enquiry revealed the fact that the Chinese sold retail at the same price as he bought wholesale. His profit was made from the fact that he had a few months' credit with the manufacturer and that he was able to make profitable use of the cases in which the goods were delivered! Needless to say he captured the market, had a very large turnover and cut out his Japanese competitor. Such cases could be multiplied all over the Orient, and when it comes to competition with the Westerners, the shoe pinches even more—for us!

Some people still seem to think that behind an immobile face and an unhurried manner the Chinese merchant hides a lack of enterprise and initiative which will always leave him an easy prey to the hustlers from the West. This is very far from the truth. Chinese buyers have been handicapped in the past in competing with foreign traders because

WHY DISCUSS CHINA ?

they have often not known the ropes or commanded the credit as did their competitors. But this disability is quickly passing. The Chinese compradore is the most essential factor in the success of the firms that do business in China. He is necessary for securing orders in China and generally for pushing the interests of the concern locally. But the time is rapidly coming when he will oust the foreign business man, or at least seriously challenge his supremacy. He has learned our side of the game more quickly than we have learned his. He will be able to dispense with his employer much more easily than his employer can dispense with him. His enterprise and initiative will then be manifest to the world, as they already are to all who have had personal dealings with him. If he can at the same time maintain the high standard of business integrity for which he is famous and secure the confidence of investors in China, there will be a complete reversal of the economic positions of foreigner and Chinese within a generation. Indeed, it is no exaggeration to say that this process has already begun and is proceeding rapidly. To think of the Chinese as our inferiors, even in our own game, is a very big mistake.

But the significance of China's size is not only to be seen when we consider her people as colonizers and men of business enterprise. They are a nation amazingly unified in life and thought, with a tenacity of purpose and a quiet strength which seems almost uncanny to us of the modern mind. Some years before the Revolution which overthrew the Manchu dynasty a friend of mine was travelling in a remote part of China, and fell in with an ancient scholar who told him the following tale of the early days of that dynasty. When the Manchus found themselves in possession of the country by right of conquest, they realized that they needed Chinese to help them in governing it. They therefore called certain leading Chinese statesmen to help them in framing laws and constitution. One of these suggested the plan that the Chinese should be the workers and traders, and that the Manchus should be established as the national guard, with a garrison in each large town. He therefore proposed that they should draw pensions for their services as defenders of the nation. When challenged as to this proposal by his Chinese friends, who considered that he had placed the Manchu yoke in perpetuity upon the neck of the Chinese and caused the latter to support their conquerors in power and idleness, he is reported to have replied, " Do not fear ; I have made this plan in such a way that within three hundred years our present conquerors will be destitute, begging bread from door to door." I cannot vouch for the legend, but it bears the stamp of truth, and within a few years of its recital to my friend the prophecy was literally fulfilled. The Manchu dynasty lasted from 1644–1911. One of the chief causes of its decay was the idleness and luxury of the Manchus, and their present desperate state is due to the fact that for the most part they don't know how to do an honest day's work.

It is with a people who can take long views, who know how to wait, who have the patience to hold on against all adversity, and who have a knack of coming to the front again in time after every reverse —it is with such people that we Westerners have to deal—we, the impatient, the short-sighted—so keen on our quick-returns and our quack remedies.

Few foreigners in China can compare with Dr. Arthur H. Smith in his profound and sympathetic understanding of Chinese character. He told me how, when at a dinner in New York, a lady turned to him and said, " Dr. Smith, after all your knowledge

WHY DISCUSS CHINA? 21

of China, what would you say is the leading Chinese characteristic?" "I do not know," he said, "that I have ever been asked exactly that question before, but I think I should say it was reasonableness." Turning to Mr. Rockhill, for many years American minister in Peking, who was sitting on her other side, the lady repeated the remark and asked his opinion. "Yes," he said, "after my life in China, though I might not have put it in that way myself, I believe Dr. Smith is right." Going back to China after the years of war and so-called peace, wherein the madness of Europe had so fearfully revealed itself, one could not fail to be impressed again with this characteristic. "Li," or reason, right, the proper thing, is one of the great Chinese words. To describe a thing as "wu li" without reason, is to condemn it utterly. To say that a certain course has "li" is to give it the highest possible commendation. Time and again the appeal to reason and to humour works with a group of Chinese where nothing else will, and where bullying or domineering simply enrages your man and loses your case for you. One morning travelling by chair across Szechwan a snowstorm in the night induced in my coolies a great desire for bed the next day. I was told that they were on strike and had no intentions of moving for twenty-four hours. I sent them a polite message explaining that I had to reach my destination at a certain time, and that if they chose to make several very strenuous forced marches on the following days, I would be glad to give them the day's rest. Within an hour we were on our way cheerful and laughing as we plunged through the snow-covered fields, and we reached our destination in time. I know what a different story I should have had to tell had I tried threats. Such a tale can be told by every traveller in China who has ever appealed to reason in dealing with the common man.

When to these outstanding qualities we add industry and endurance far beyond the normal in the West, adaptability learnt through generations of living in close proximity in the patriarchal homestead, resourcefulness that amounts to genius, a peace-loving temper and a real reverence for learning, we have a combination of qualities that make the mere size of China seem a small thing compared with the vigour and possibilities of her citizens. It is such a people whose mass is now but beginning to be felt in the life of the world. When Western nations battered down the barriers that shut off China from the rest of mankind in order that they might open up her markets and draw revenue from her wealth, they were bringing into the community of nations a factor far more important than they realized for the life of the generations still unborn. Commerce, transport facilities, interchange of ideas, political relationships, are combining to increase the influence of China in the world. It becomes a matter of immense moment to consider what that influence is and may become.

There is no element in the Great Society at once so unknown and so hopeful for human progress as China. Through many centuries she has matured her thought and learned many lessons in the art of living. She has been preserved, as it were, in isolation or comparative isolation, and now she comes suddenly into an alien world desperately needing some of the treasures she brings. Before we enter upon the consideration of the conflict of civilizations, let us take time to appreciate the nature of this treasure, or at least to see how we may appreciate it.

CHAPTER II

THE TREASURES OF THE PAST.

NOTHING could be more foolish than to imagine that one could epitomize in one short chapter the distinctive elements in a civilization achieved through thousands of years, the product of many minds and lives. What I can do, perhaps, is to give a few indications of the kind of study needed to get into the spirit of old China, to give a key that may unlock some doors of the treasure-house.

It has been well said that ". people coming to China with the idea that the Chinese are a people to be civilized can never hope to get beneath the surface of things. They cannot see in Chinese culture anything that possesses spiritual worth." Happily this attitude of cultural superiority is beginning to give way, but anyone who has lived in the Far East knows that it is still very far from having disappeared. Wherever it appears, in social intercourse, in commercial or political life, or in missionary propaganda, it is fatal to a true mutual understanding and therefore to any real solution of the race question. This attitude must be replaced by one of respect, by humble and painstaking enquiry and by the effort to sympathize with and understand a civilization so very different from our own. Such respect must not be a mere washy sentiment; it must be won by each of us for himself as we discover those things which call forth and deserve respect.

I would suggest in the first place a study of Chinese

art, and the crafts which arise out of it, including the making of pottery, cloisonné, lacquers and rugs, the type of architecture developed in China, the carvings in ivory, jade and wood, the weaving of tapestries, brocades and silks. To stand before some of the paintings that have come down to us from the T'ang and Sung dynasties (618–907 and 960–1127 A.D. respectively) is to appreciate the fact that the Chinese of those periods had a wonderful sense of the beautiful, a great power of expressing it, and an amazing appreciation of its significance. It was Hsieh Ho who lived towards the end of the fifth century (A.D.) who propounded the famous canons of art:

" 1. Rhythmic vitality;
" 2. Organic structure;
" 3. Conformity with nature;
" 4. Appropriate colouring;
" 5. Arrangement, which means that one recognizes the ever-living mission of painting to tell that nature provides the experiences of the soul; and
" 6. Transmission of classic models."

Over two hundred painters seem to have attained to eminence during the T'ang dynasty, and many of their works have come down to us. The landscapes of this period are full of life, and we also have a number of portraits and studies. The Sung paintings are perhaps more remarkable for their simplicity and force, an idea revealed in a few telling strokes. The power of Chinese art lies in its feeling. The artist was taught never to paint anything unless he could, while doing so, experience the emotions proper to that subject. We can enter into these emotions as we study a Chinese masterpiece, almost feel the power of the hurricane as we gaze on bamboos in the wind, or enter into the

THE TREASURES OF THE PAST 25

magical stillness of the autumn night as we look at the picture of the moon shining on the waters of the lake. The men who made these things have come down to us, in their warm affection for nature,[1] in their subtle appreciation of beauty and humour. They were the children of a civilization already hoary with age before the Norman Conquest. They have bequeathed to us something by which we can, if we will, enter into their spirit, and, as it were, touch their delicate and skilful hands. In the study of Chinese art we can clearly see one of the characteristics of Chinese civilization. To the Greek, man was the centre of the picture, and the noblest examples of his art are seen in the presentation of the human form. To the Chinese, man was as nothing in the midst of the wonderful and beautiful universe he inhabits. A characteristic Chinese painting will show two friends, it may be, contemplating a beautiful sunset. The men are but a suggestion that the sunset can be appreciated by the mind and can enrich the friendship, but the point of the picture is not in the figures; it is in the fact that the world of nature speaks a language. The never-ending flow of the waterfall, the piled masses of rugged rock, the perfect shapeliness of the ancient tree, even the grotesque or absurd in nature were a witness to a spirit, no less sure a token than the driven leaves which tell us of the power of the wind. Man is a very small item in the landscape: but at least he has eyes with which he may see and a heart which may beat with the eternal purpose.

To breathe the spirit of ancient China we need also to come under the spell of her beautiful buildings. The site is chosen with a sure eye to

[1] The collection in the old Winter Palace, Peking, is especially noteworthy in this connection.

effect, the arrangement gives one a chance to take in their characteristic features, and space is allowed so that they have no sense of being suffocated by surrounding buildings as is so often the case in the West. The roofs of brilliant green or blue or gold, with the glazed tiles reflecting the noonday sun, with their corners turned up towards heaven, with the quaint ornamentation on roof-beam and gable; the giant pillars and mighty beams on which these roofs are supported; the marble steps leading up to stately porches built regardless of any niggard economy of space—these are some of the things that impress the foreigner and make him realize that this type of beauty has sprung out a life in some very important respects different from that which created our Gothic cathedrals or even the Taj Mahal. If you see in architecture the expression of what a people has achieved in thought and of what are its hopes and aspirations, you cannot fail to recognize both that China has something of real value and that it is something quite distinctive, her own product which we need insight and sympathy to understand and learn from. We cannot enter the precincts of the Imperial City, where now are so fittingly housed some of the finest specimens of Chinese arts and crafts, nor can we visit some of the ancient temples of China, without a sense of respect and even reverence for those who have put themselves into this majesty and beauty.

It is impossible to dwell on other aspects of the art life of China. It is a world of its own, and I invite you to enter it, sure that it will yield a rich reward in itself, and also that it will prove at least the threshold to the understanding of this people whose destinies are bound up with ours in the West for good or ill.

A second deep well from which we must draw

THE TREASURES OF THE PAST

if we are to enter into the spirit of old China is her literature. It is unnecessary to insist that it can only be fully appreciated if read in the original, but this is even more true of Chinese than of, say, Greek or Latin literature. The Chinese language is a thing apart. Its characters, each of which represents an idea rather than a word, baffle one by their number and complexity. Yet in many of them a whole world of meaning and allusion is bound up. What they suggest to the ripe Chinese scholar no foreign student may wholly understand. They are associated with passages of beauty and nobility. There is distilled into them the fragrance of many a pithy saying of the sages. They scintillate like a distant star whose light started on its voyage to your eye some thousands of years before you were born. The Chinese reverence the written word as no other race. Scraps of paper with characters inscribed on them must be preserved with care or destroyed with decorum. Each character is like a living person, aged and reverent, having a personality of its own. It is in such characters that the thoughts of past generations have been transmitted to us. Confucius himself (born 550 or 551 B.C.) was a collector of ancient learning, and disclaimed any idea of originality. The wisdom of China seems to come direct and almost unchanged from days when men acted more on intuition than from thought-out reasons. Yet it represents, without doubt, a world of hard-won experience condensed into telling phrases. Like Chinese art, it leaves much to the imagination. Three or four characters cannot be adequately translated into less than a dozen words, and even then we often seem rather to be standing on the brink of a thought than bathing ourselves in its depths.

In spite of this difficulty of adequate translation,

it is well worth while to read the classics in English. I would advise reading such translations for oneself, and not relying too much on any interpretations of their spirit by others. I shall have to come back to some of the fundamental ideas of Chinese philosophy in later lectures, but there are one or two things I should like to say at once, somewhat by way of introduction and caution.

We need to be very careful about reading into Chinese writings purely Western ideas. Doing this has resulted in an over-emphasis on certain aspects of the classics and a failure to appreciate others. Let me take one example. It is very often stated that the teachings of the great sages contain practically nothing on the spiritual side of man's nature, and are almost exclusively devoted to the ethical. The saying of Confucius, " We do not know life ; how then can we know death ? " is often quoted, or that other remark about him in the Analects, " The subjects on which the master did not talk, were prodigies, feats of strength, disorder, and spiritual beings." Yet, even the teachings of Confucius are permeated by the sense of a divine order which must be observed in human affairs. That is to say, there is a reference of all life to something eternal to a standard of absolute value. He says explicitly " the life of the moral man is an exemplification of the universal moral order. The life of the vulgar person, on the other hand, is a contradiction of the universal moral order." Though there is recurring emphasis on moral precepts and the outward life, there is a recognition of something deeper, as where he says, " The men of olden times who studied virtue had only their inner development in view ; those who study it now have an eye to the applause of others." It is no outward idea of morality that will satisfy this great moralist. Still more

THE TREASURES OF THE PAST

when we turn to Lao Tze or Mencius or to Meh Tze do we get the idea of an inner life nourished by relation to some deeper springs, some abiding principle of goodness and love. While, therefore, this aspect of life which we call the spiritual or religious, the sense of mystic communion with the divine Being, is not expressed in the language with which we are familiar, I cannot myself doubt that the real experience is there, and I believe a sympathetic reading of the classics does not support the common view that the best Chinese thought is sceptical in regard to God. It is reverent and guarded. It conveys its deepest thoughts by hints rather than explicitly. It will not venture to dogmatize. It distrusts the blatantly supernatural, preferring to see the true meaning of life in the normal rather than in the abnormal. Not looking to any supreme revelation of God in a Person, it has not clothed God with personal attributes, but it has patiently sought to understand the words that He has spoken in the book of nature, in men's relationships with one another, and in the deepest recesses of the human heart.

The second suggestion I have to make about reading the Chinese classics is this—that we allow our imagination full play. This must, of course, be guided by a knowledge of historical setting and such study of Chinese life as may be possible. But in many of the sayings of the sages we have not a treatise but a suggestion. The teachers of old China had the same pedagogic instinct that is so wonderfully exemplified in the teaching of Christ. He taught in parables, gave hints, which those only who had ears could hear and those who had eyes see. There is need of the same kind of insight if we are to see the inner meaning of many of the words of the Chinese sages. I used to read the classics with a Chinese teacher, a man of rare simplicity of life who had never before been in touch with a Christian. Repeatedly we discussed the differences and similarities of The Great Learning and the Gospels. Always he was concerned to show how Christian truth had already been expressed in this volume of concentrated wisdom, till one day when I found myself arguing for a reading of a certain passage in conformity with Christian thought he said in effect, "Yes, it might mean that, but no commentator has seen that meaning, and I doubt if it were really intended by the writer." Shortly afterwards I visited his home and he asked his little boy to repeat to me the prayer that he had taught him. It was a simple child's prayer, but my attention was arrested by the following request, "Grant us the gift of Thy Holy Spirit to illuminate the writings of Scripture and of the Chinese classics." We need to bring the same power of spiritual insight and inspired imagination to the one as to the other. I am not saying that they are of equal spiritual worth, for with all my respect for the Chinese classics I cannot find in them the wealth of spiritual truth and the full revelation of God that I find in the Bible. But we in the West who have so poorly followed the one, have much to learn from the other, and the right kind of study will bring rich rewards.

Chinese literature is not, of course, confined to philosophy. Recent translations have enabled English readers to gain some idea of the beauty of Chinese verse. Few realize the wealth of such literature in China. It is on record that during the T'ang dynasty no less than nine hundred volumes of poetry were issued by various authors, and the total number of poems fell little short of fifty thousand! Whatever the literary merit of such a gigantic output may have been, at least it suggests a considerable interest in

THE TREASURES OF THE PAST

poetic composition and a certain reading public. The poetry which has been preserved has a delicacy, a reserve and a fineness of feeling which give it a high rank among the literary productions of the world. It is unfortunate that it is so very difficult to carry over its peculiar flavour and charm into any other language.

History again takes a large place in Chinese literature, though here I am afraid it must be confessed that the bulk is more impressive than the historical insight of the writers. There has been but little attempt in China to interpret the meaning of events, while the number recorded is so huge as to give the student a sense of being snowed under, and unable to distinguish between the significant and the insignificant. However, the patience and attention to detail of the Chinese chroniclers is beyond dispute. The raw materials have been preserved for future use.

Leaving the more deliberate products of Chinese thought, we may consider the structure of Chinese society as a revelation of the genius of the nation. It would be well to read books written before the influences of the West had produced such marked changes in the social organism. A volume like Dr. A. H. Smith's *Village Life in China* introduces one to a civilization expressed in many time-honoured customs, in the large patriarchal family, in the theatrical performance, in the customs of the market, in the secret society, and in the trade guild. Here again we want eyes that we may see the deeper significance of the facts. Chinese society is very closely knit together, notwithstanding the appearances to the contrary, in recent fighting and disputing. In the family home, often according to our ideas terribly overcrowded, you have several generations living together and learning, as one follows another, the art of getting as much happiness out of life as is possible under unfavourable circumstances, and the still harder art of living peaceably with persons of different temperaments, ages and interests, in a very close association. Of course, there are plenty of quarrels in Chinese homes, as there are all over the world, but the family holds together notwithstanding, and in adversity shows a surprising sense of mutual responsibility and coherence. In the trade guilds and in the provincial guilds we have examples of democratic organization and of co-operation of a peculiarly complete kind. I shall have to refer to these in more detail when we consider industrial questions, but I want chiefly to point out here that the genius of the people can be studied and appreciated in these forms of popular voluntary association far more than in the State organization. The political power in China has until recently been largely in the hands of the few, sometimes enlightened sovereigns and sometimes tyrants or incompetent rascals. The real power has been with the people. Mencius taught quite explicitly the right of rebellion. " The people are the most important element in a country, and the ruler is lightest," was his maxim, to which he holds tenaciously with all its consequences. He sees clearly the need of differing functions in the body politic, and argues cleverly and successfully against Hên Hing, who pleaded in his day, somewhat as Gandhi is pleading in India to-day, for a return to a simpler undifferentiated life where each would do his own work. It is in the life of the people, in their relations with one another and in the theory of society that lies behind this that we discover the clue to their deepest thought.

Everyone knows that Chinese social theory is based upon the " Five Relations." In the Doctrine

THE TREASURES OF THE PAST

of the Mean we have it stated in these words : " The duties of universal obligation are five and the virtues wherewith they are practised are three. The duties are those between sovereign and minister, between father and son, between husband and wife, between elder brother and younger brother, and those belonging to the intercourse of friends. Those five are the duties of universal obligation. Knowledge, magnanimity and energy, these three are the virtues universally binding. And the means by which they carry the duties into practice is singleness." It is in the carrying out of the simplest duties in ordinary human intercourse that a man becomes qualified for the highest responsibility. The supreme duty of singleness of purpose is attainable by any man, however humble. The genius of China may be said to be the genius of the ordinary man, the worthwhileness of the commonplace. Therefore, China is not to be judged mainly by her sages, although these men owe their pre-eminence largely to the fact that they embody the characteristics of the race and express them in fit language. Nor is it to be judged by the feats of great generals or the reigns of outstanding sovereigns. To touch the heart of China we must understand the common people, see how they live, hear the proverbs that pass from lip to lip, study the village and clan life, enter the family and the guild. This is no easy prescription. Yet if we can in some measure follow it we shall find not that reverence for the art and literature of China grows less, but rather that we gain a deeper respect for the Chinese along with a truer understanding of the fine flowers of literature, philosophy or art.

I cannot close this consideration of the deeper side of Chinese life without taking you with me to the Altar of Heaven. As we stand there on that

34 CHINA IN THE FAMILY OF NATIONS

simple marble platform open to the winds of heaven, we remember the impressive ceremony that for centuries was the one annual expression of the nation's unity in God. The Emperor, as the Son of Heaven, came on behalf of all the people, and in their name, to make the one sacrifice to the Supreme Ruler from whom all derive life and to whom all must turn. Looking up into the vast dome of heaven with its myriad stars he offered the homage of the millions of the Celestial Empire. It was the simple expression of a primeval faith, a relic of the monotheism which in practical life for most Chinese has been supplanted by the worship of the Gods of the Buddhist pantheon. To stand on that altar, to uncover one's head and silently to absorb the meaning of that national act is to find oneself lifted out of the petty and the personal, and brought into relation to the mighty currents that have swept down the ages from some dim and unrecorded past, that have carried the countless multitudes of China to their present place in the life of the world. These currents are the blending of a divine and age-long purpose with the many wills of men and women who have been working out in pain or joy their individual destinies and shaping, though they knew it not, the destiny of one of the greatest races of mankind, certain to change in many ways the life and thought of all other races just as she is herself being changed by their life and thought to-day.

Our task in these pages will be to look at one little piece of this story where different currents begin to mix and meet, where the interchange of thought and customs is producing a new synthesis. Creation comes through the meeting and mixing of different strains or persons. New civilizations have been created in the past through such conjunc-

THE TREASURES OF THE PAST

tions. No one can say what the product of the meeting of China and the West may be. It is, in my view, the most interesting speculation in regard to the future that can engage our thought. But it is more than this. It is an issue that will mean more than any of us can guess for good or ill for ourselves, or, at least, for our children. The more people there are who can face this problem intelligently and sympathetically and who will throw their weight into the right handling of the many subsidiary problems involved, the better for humanity. I hope that what I have written in this volume will help to create many such persons. But no information here given will avail much unless the reader begins with real respect, and, at least, with the honest attempt to understand China. That is a step each must take for himself.

36 CHINA IN THE FAMILY OF NATIONS

CHART TO SHOW OUTSTANDING DATES IN CHINESE HISTORY.

	DYNASTIES.	PERSONS, ETC.
2200 B.C. — 2356, 2205	Age of Yao and Shun	
2000	Hsia Dynasty	
1800		
1766		
1600		
1400	Shang Dynasty	
1200		
1122		
1000		
800		
	Chou Dynasty	
600		Lao Tze, 604
		Confucius, 551
		Meh Tze — Age of the Great Philosophers.
		Mencius, 372
400		Seun King
249 / 206	Ch'in Dynasty	Ch'in Shih Hwang Ti (Emperor)
200		Mission of Chang Chien, 139
....	Han Dynasty	Introduction of Buddhism, 65
200 A.D. — 224 / 265	Three Kingdoms	Toleration of Buddhism, 335
400 — 420	Tsin Dynasty	
600	Interregnum	
618		
800	T'ang Dynasty	Nestorian Christianity, 634
907		Mohammedan influence begins
		Persecution of Buddhists, 845
1000 — 960	Sung Dynasty	Wang Nu Shih, 1070
1127		Chu Hsi
1200 — 1275 / 1368	Yuen (Tartar) Dynasty	Kublai Khan, Marco Polo
1400		
	Ming Dynasty	Jesuit influence begins
1600 — 1644		K'ang Hsi, 1661
1800	Ch'ing (Manchu) Dynasty	Ch'ien Lung, 1735
		Protestant Missions begin
1911	Chinese Republic	

NOTE.—The above dates and persons are a selection chosen to make clear the text. The left hand column is over simplified, many of the lesser Dynasties being purposely omitted and the dates given are in several cases only approximate. Dates opposite a person give his birth (approximately) in the case of a philosopher, the commencement of a reign in the case of an Emperor.

CHAPTER III

EARLY INTERNATIONAL CONNECTIONS
(BEFORE 1840)

I HAVE tried in the previous chapter to give some picture of the Chinese and their ancient civilization in order that the reader might realize as vividly as possible the nature of the problems created by the entrance of this great people into the Family of Nations. I shall now trace the earlier connections between China and the rest of the world so as to supply some historical background for our consideration of China's present relations with other states.

It is commonly supposed that China has, throughout her long history, been cut off from intercourse with the rest of the world, and, as a broad generalization this statement is good enough. But it will be worth while for our purpose to note the periods in Chinese history when there was some degree of mutual intercourse, what may be called, if you wish, the "exceptions that prove the rule."

Chinese history is generally regarded as beginning in the twenty-fourth century B.C. with the reigns of the great Emperors Yao and Shun.[1] This is spoken of as the Golden Age of China, semi-mythical, no doubt, but probably with some basis of fact. These two emperors, who reigned in immediate succession, have been chiefly admired for their high

[1] Others regard Fu Hsi (2852 B.C.) as at least semi-historical.

personal qualities, no doubt exaggerated by the praise bestowed on them by Confucius and his disciples. Yao is reputed to have revised the calendar and given it the form which has been used until almost the present time. In his days we are told that there was such a degree of security in the country that men never locked the doors of their houses! So far as is known, there was no intercourse with the West in those far-off days. The empire was probably confined to quite a small area in the basin of the Yellow River, which seems to have been the birth-place of Chinese civilization.

The more strictly historical records date from the rise of the Chou dynasty (placed somewhere between 1120 and 1050 B.C.), and from this period onwards we have records for upwards of 3,000 years, which can be regarded as fairly accurate, and in many cases they are actually contemporary. During the Chou dynasty, which lasted over 800 years, the great philosophers of China flourished; and it was during this time that many of the political and social customs were started which continued almost unbroken till the foundation of the Republic in 1911, or even still continue to the present day.

The student of international affairs may note, in passing, that it was during this period (to be exact in 546 B.C.), that we find the first authentic record of a league of nations, in which no fewer than fourteen states met together to enter into a covenant to bring wars to an end. It is told of Hsiang Hsü, the originator of the scheme, that he moved in the matter in order "to stop the wars of the barons and also to make a name for himself"! The first object failed lamentably; as to the second, I cannot presume to decide. The historian in giving a good many pages to the account of the effort and the ceremonies connected therewith, says, " Chung-ni made me insert this ceremony because of the many speeches for which it afforded the opportunity." The spirit in which the matter was taken up may be judged by the action of the Prime Minister of the leading state of Ch'in, who, when approached, seems to have followed the advice of a colleague who said, "War is a calamity for the people ; a blight on all economical administration and a great disaster for small states. Now, when a man comes with a plan for stopping war, even though we may think it can't be done, we ought to let him try. Besides, suppose you do not take the matter up, well, then, Ch'u will. She will straightway call the barons together, and thereby our position amongst the lords as primus is gone." When the day came for signing the covenant of this ancient league, the representatives of the state of Ch'u arrived, wearing their armour under their ceremonial clothes ; and so tense was the situation that the representatives of Ch'in were only reassured by the recollection that they were next to the city gate, and if attacked could readily escape within the city walls !

The speech of Hsiang Hsü is the one that seems most worthy of being preserved, for when the mutual suspicion was brought to his notice, and especially the concealed armour, he remarked, " No harm can come to us from such a thing as this. Even a common peasant cannot get along without trusting and being trusted. The outcome is death. Nothing can be gained by lack of trust at a meeting of the barons. I have never been troubled at any notion that men could 'eat their words' and not suffer for doing so. We come together because we trust each other. One of us shows he is not fit to be trusted. Well, that hurts him, not me." If our sentiments have not advanced very greatly since those days, nearly 2500 years ago, let us hope that our achievements may, and that Geneva may prove a stronger bulwark to peace than did the covenant that was signed at Sung in the year 546 B.C. The incident is chiefly interesting as showing that there were some people in ancient China who tried to put their peace principles into practice at a time when the whole country was distracted by war.

Passing over three centuries during which the great Chinese philosophers flourished, we may pause a moment to think of Ch'in Shih Hwang Ti, the builder of the Great Wall of China and founder of the Ch'in dynasty B.C. 221. This Emperor combined the petty states into which China had broken up with the decay of the Chou dynasty, and abolished the feudal system which he regarded as a chief source of China's weakness and internal dissensions. He was bitterly opposed by the literati, who could quote endless passages from the classics in support of the *status quo*. The Emperor determined to put an end to such nonsense, and the result is that his name has been handed down to posterity as the arch-vandal who destroyed the classical records. All books except works on agriculture, medicine and divination had to be brought to the nearest official and burnt. As a matter of fact, public libraries and official records were excluded from the decree, and it is probable that no great loss was suffered. It may well have been terribly irritating to a vigorous reformer to have ancient writings perpetually quoted against him, and I, for one, am not disposed to blame him nearly as much as the historians, who, naturally enough, took the part of the literati against the Emperor. Unfortunately, when he found the burning of the classics ineffective as a means of closing the mouths of these reactionary pedants, he proceeded a step

EARLY INTERNATIONAL CONNECTIONS 41

further and caused 460 of them to be buried alive. This act we need not seek to excuse! The Great Wall was built in order to keep out the invasions from the north by the Hsiang-nu, who seem to have belonged to some stock of the Huns, and it has stood in subsequent generations as a parable to show China's attitude towards other nations. This also is hardly fair to the Emperor Ch'in Shih or to China generally, for there is no doubt that these northern invaders were far less civilized than the Chinese of that day, and were a real menace extremely hard to deal with.

It is of especial interest that during this epoch the teachings of the Chinese philosopher Seun King were largely accepted in preference to those of Confucius and Mencius. This sage held that all men were by nature bad, and that peace could only be achieved through fear. Ch'in Shih Hwang Ti, in following his teaching, carried out many very severe sentences on his subjects. A picture of the court of that day shows a man kneeling before the Emperor, and two executioners standing at the side evidently waiting their chance as soon as the petitioner has finished! Chin Shih Hwang Ti believed that he could found a dynasty that would rule for ever, that history was to begin anew with himself, and that by violence and domineering he could secure peace. He did for a brief period establish his rule over all the smaller states, but his dynasty lasted less than fifty years, the shortest on record, and the judgment of China upon him is that his method was a signal failure. One thing has lasted from the dynasty—the name China—which is probably probably derived from the word Ch'in.

The earliest authentic record of foreign influence in China dates roughly from the beginning of our era, when Buddhism was first introduced. About one hundred years earlier a mission was sent West by the Emperor Wu Ti (of the Han dynasty, B.C. 140-87), and news was obtained of the powerful nation known to the Chinese as Yüeh Ti, who then inhabited the area now known as Bokhara. Chinese products were being sold there as Indian goods, having arrived from that direction. This mission accomplished little in the way of opening up trade as the two peoples were still separated by the barbarous Hsiang-nu.

The date B.C. 6 is given for the first translations of Buddhist writings into Chinese, but it was not until A.D. 65 that Buddhism was introduced into China in any large way. It is said that the Emperor Ming Ti had a dream in which he saw a giant who bade him send messengers to the West. The messengers were sent, and returned with two Buddhist priests from India. One can speculate as to what might have been the course of history had they proceeded still further West and come back with two of the apostles of Christ!

The form of Buddhism introduced into China was what is known as northern Buddhism in marked distinction to the southern Buddhism practised in Ceylon. While the new faith was born in another country, and had all the disadvantages of being a foreign one, opposed in certain particulars to Chinese ideas, it became in course of time strongly infiltrated with these ideas, and is now not less influential among the common people in China than the indigenous religions. After its first introduction, Buddhism suffered a severe reverse amounting almost to an eclipse, but by 335 A.D. the new religion had gained such hold that the ruling emperor issued a decree of complete religious toleration, allowing Chinese for the first time to enter the Buddhist priesthood. Chinese pilgrims travelled frequently

EARLY INTERNATIONAL CONNECTIONS 43

to India, and a succession of Indian monks, some of whom had great influence, came into China. Most of the Buddhist books are translations of Indian *sûtras*. In the year 845 the Taoists succeeded in bringing about a terrible persecution of the Buddhists, when 4,600 monasteries were destroyed and 260,000 monks and nuns were driven into civil life. This is one of the very few instances of religious persecution in Chinese history, and may be compared to the Boxer uprising in 1900-1. The effort in each case was short-lived and followed by a reaction. There can be no doubt that the religious fellowship established between India and China was one of the chief, if not the chief, means of opening up intercourse between China and the outside world until about a century ago. I believe that Buddhism owes its success in China to the fact that Chinese philosophies have been so negative and reserved in regard to spiritual realities, and that there is something in the Chinese, as well as in all other peoples, that seeks for communion with God. Ancestor worship cannot take the place of the worship of the Supreme Being. Buddhism in China has supplied, especially in the worship of Kwang Yin (the Goddess of Mercy), something which answers the craving of the human heart for an assurance of response from the unseen world.[1]

Be that as it may, what we are now considering is rather the effect of the intercourse with India made possible through the Buddhist incursion. It can be shown that Indian ideas influenced in many ways the architecture, arithmetic, literature, and music of China, besides other branches of art and science. In part, this influence was transitory.

[1] It has also been maintained that Buddhism was adopted partly for political reasons, especially because it gives a religious sanction to the idea of retribution, an idea opposed by the Confucian scholars.

For example, the Chinese syllabary, introduced by Indians in order to facilitate their work of translation, is now only preserved in Chinese dictionaries, although for some time it was very generally used.[1] The same is true of the literary style which was then introduced, was all the fashion for several centuries, and then fell into disuetude.

In these particulars, then, we may say that the influence of India was for a time a very important fact in the life of China. Its permanent mark on Chinese thought and social life has been much less than might have been expected. China has a way of reasserting herself. She comes back to the Tao, her own inner nature, even though slowly—a fact to be borne in mind in considering her future in the light of present events.

To what extent did Græco-Roman civilization affect China in these early days ? There is evidence of trade in silk with Greece, and the Roman Empire was known to the Chinese in the second century A.D. as Ta Chin, the Emperor Marcus Aurelius having apparently sent envoys to Cochin China to open up trade. It is probable that some Greek influences reached China through India. Again in the seventh century the Emperor Theodosius sent an ambassador to the Chinese court. There is no evidence that this intercourse had any deep influence on China. One may say broadly that the Græco-Roman culture which has so largely shaped our modern European world had no share in the formative forces which have combined to make China what she is to-day.

The one notable exception to this is the influence of early Christian missions. The first introduction of the Christian faith seems to have been by a Syrian

[1] The modern phonetic script is a new thing and cannot be spoken of as a revival of the old idea of a syllabary introduced by Buddhist monks.

EARLY INTERNATIONAL CONNECTIONS 45

monk named Olopan during the reign of the most illustrious monarch of the T'ang dynasty T'ai T'sung (not to be confounded with the first Manchu Emperor of the same name). This was in the year 634. Much favour was shown to him and he was permitted to build churches. The only record we have of this introduction of Christianity is the famous Nestorian tablet (discovered in 1623). There can be no question of its authenticity, and the record certainly suggests a fairly widespread adoption of the Christian faith. History is silent as to the reasons which led to the decline and final extinction of Nestorian Christianity. The tablet was engraved nearly 150 years after the arrival of Olopan, and at that time there must have been a number of flourishing churches. It is to be hoped that some day materials may be discovered which will help to solve what is at present a curious mystery.

To religious enthusiasm, in the first place, is also due another movement that has affected the life of China. In the early days of the Muslim faith China was marked out as a land to be won. About the end of the seventh century there seems to have been an attempt to reach China with a military expedition in the interests of Islam, but this failed. Through commercial approaches in the south the new faith began to influence Canton; but little progress seems to have been made during the T'ang dynasty. It was not until the beginning of the 13th century that, during the Mongol dynasty, there was a large influx of Arab traders who brought their religion with them. While Mohammedanism has taken hold of a considerable number of the Chinese people, and is specially strong in certain provinces, notably in Kansu, I do not think that it can be said to have exerted any very considerable influence upon Chinese thought or customs.

46 CHINA IN THE FAMILY OF NATIONS

It may be well before passing on to the later periods to remind ourselves of the place which China held at the time of the T'ang dynasty (618–907 A.D.). By the Chinese generally this period is regarded as one of unique splendour and success. China was for three hundred years under purely Chinese rulers. On the whole, they were enlightened and far-seeing men. Their rule was extended to Korea in the north and to Canton in the south, and even Persia sought help from China. It has been suggested that the country then became an asylum for peoples who were elsewhere being persecuted for their faith, and that some of these brought with them arts and crafts hitherto unknown to the Chinese. Mr. Wells Williams says that China during the T'ang period was " probably the most civilized country on earth ; the darkest days of the West, when Europe was wrapped in the ignorance and degradation of the Middle Ages, formed the brightest era of the East."

About the time of the Norman Conquest, China, having passed through a period of complete disorganization, when she was overrun by hordes of barbarians, was reduced to the old expedient of buying off her enemies by huge gifts amounting to as much as an annual " present " of 250,000 ounces of silver, 250,000 pieces of silk and 250,000 catties of tea. It is small wonder that the country was reduced to the verge of bankruptcy. From this she was saved by the energy and statesmanship of Wang An Shih, who is sometimes spoken of as the pioneer of State Socialism. This description is not very accurate, for his reforms really depended upon a strong central government, and were carried out against the persistent opposition of many of the people. They included a system of State loans to farmers, income tax to take the place of the

EARLY INTERNATIONAL CONNECTIONS 47

older corvée, and nationalization of commerce. A militia Act was also introduced calling for every family with more than two males to supply one in time of war for the army and one in time of peace for the police force. Wang's enemies used the appearance of a comet, which was attributed to his reforming zeal, as a means of displacing him. But when the comet disappeared without doing any serious damage, the Emperor, who had always trusted him, was able to reinstate him in office!

The modern history of China is regarded as commencing with the Mongol dynasty under Kublai Khan. It is difficult to give an exact date for the commencement of the Mongol supremacy in China, as during a number of years the Mongols were engaged in the gradual subjugation of the various states into which what is now China proper was then divided. The Mongols, though far inferior in culture to the Chinese, were at this time a people with a written language and with a sufficient appreciation of art and literature to seek to preserve it. It has been said of Kublai that he conquered China only in turn to be conquered by it. Trade with the West was extensive during his reign, and he introduced on a large scale a paper currency, based first upon silk, then upon silver, and finally upon copper. The depreciation of this currency was one of the causes of the downfall of the dynasty. During this period the novel and the drama were introduced into China, where they have since had a great vogue. This is perhaps the most considerable gift that came to China from the outside during the Mongol régime, and it seems to have come from the Tartars rather than from the Mongols themselves.

It may be well here to speak briefly of the early relations between China and Japan. We must go back to the reign of Ch'in Shih Hwang Ti for our first reference to the sister nation. It is recorded that he sent out several expeditions into the Yellow Sea to discover an island supposed to be the home of the genii. One of these, headed by a certain Hsü Fu, contained, we are told, 500 boys and 500 girls and many valuable books. They set sail from Chefoo and never returned. It is supposed that he introduced Chinese civilization into Japan! Coming down to more reliable records, we find the T'ang Emperor T'ai T'sung equipping an expedition to Korea in answer to their request for deliverance from Japanese domination, the latter Power having linked themselves with one side in an internal quarrel. The expedition, after some minor successes, had to retreat in 645 A.D., this being, I suppose, the first time that Japan and China came to blows in regard to Korea. The intercourse between the two countries was not, however, confined to conflict, and during the T'ang dynasty many Japanese came over as students to China. It was then that Chinese arts and civilization came to have a dominating influence in the development of Japan.

The military ambition of Kublai Khan was stirred by accounts of Japanese wealth, and he made various efforts to secure their allegiance. The final attempt reminds one of nothing so much as the efforts of Philip of Spain to subdue another island people on the Western shores of Europe. In 1281 a fleet of 4,500 ships sailed from the ports of Fukien for Japan. Stubborn resistance and finally a terrific storm completed their discomfiture, and very few returned to tell the tale.

During the Ming dynasty there were further encounters with Japan, both in Korea and in Central China. Japanese traders and pirates were continually trying to enter Ningpo and other ports, and, on the whole, they seem to have been successful in

EARLY INTERNATIONAL CONNECTIONS 49

the military operations they undertook. But no permanent foothold was obtained in either place, and Japan had to content herself, at that time, in consolidating her own power, and giving up her continental ambitions. In the light of recent happenings it is well to remember these episodes which brought no permanent gain to either country and meant much loss to Korea and to the peoples of the coast provinces.

The Ming dynasty was also notable for intercourse with Western nations. In 1516 the first vessel flying a European flag in these waters arrived at Canton. It was Portuguese, and was favourably received and some trade was opened up. Three Portuguese settlements were established, but the treatment of the Chinese by the settlers was such that the Chinese determined to drive them out, and succeeded everywhere except in Macao, which is still held by Portugal. Spain followed suit, and seized the Philippine Islands in 1543. Their cruel treatment of the Chinese in trading with them, and also the terrible massacre of Chinese residents in Manila, was so much resented that they were not permitted to settle on the mainland. In 1622 the Dutch made an attempt to seize Amoy, but were driven out and compelled to retire to Formosa. Thus trade with the West, commenced with violence and bloodshed, was naturally distrusted by China. She did not want our merchandise at that price, and small wonder! Europe had commenced the policy of commercial aggression, and in the first encounters she had been worsted. But the inventions of James Watt, and Arkwright, and Maxim, and a host of others, were yet to make it possible for Europe to reverse the decision. How little the pioneers of applied science knew what their labours would mean for the relations of East and West, and how they would be misused by their aggressive kinsmen! It may be of interest in this connection to note that one of the gifts brought to China by the Jesuit missionaries who arrived there during the Ming dynasty (reign of Wan Li, 1573–1619) was the manufacture of certain types of firearms. Their success at this period seems to have been largely due to their scientific knowledge, and it is recorded that before the fall of the Ming dynasty no fewer than 114 members of the royal family were Christians.

The last of the great dynasties of Chinese history was again a foreign one. The Manchus attacked China at a time when the Mings had become degenerate and unworthy of high office. The palace was filled with self-seeking office-bearers; the Manchu hosts met with comparatively little opposition and found many traitors ready enough to sell their country. Again we have the phenomenon of a foreign occupation; but the Manchus differed from the Mongols in their readiness to use Chinese in many of the chief positions of responsibility. Their government of China contains some of the most illustrious names in Chinese history, notably the two great Emperors K'ang Hsi and Ch'ien Lung. As I am only trying to epitomize China's relations with foreign Powers, it is impossible to expatiate on the reigns of these great emperors. It is not without significance that two of the emperors most warmly praised by Chinese historians should have been aliens, being another indication of the fair-mindedness of the Chinese and their lack of unreasoning prejudice against foreigners.

It was during the reign of K'ang Hsi (1661–1722) that Russia first came into prominence as a force to be reckoned with in Chinese politics. Shortly before his accession a Russian embassy had arrived

EARLY INTERNATIONAL CONNECTIONS 51

in Peking to open up trade. Their goods were accepted as tribute from an inferior State, and the Emperor returned a present to show his pleasure at the loyalty of the Russians.

In 1670 China sent a mission to Moscow, but language difficulties prevented its achieving any result. A Russian mission accompanied the Chinese one when it returned, and tried to reach an agreement on frontiers and trade relations. No agreement was reached, and ultimately war broke out and was waged intermittently from 1682–1686, when K'ang Hsi asked the Dutch to act as intermediaries ; but a peace was not concluded until 1689 through the help of Jesuit missionaries. For the first, but by no means for the last time, a treaty was concluded between a European State and China in which the texts in the two languages were far from identical. One result of this treaty was the opening up of a fairly steady trade. The happy relations between Peter the Great and K'ang Hsi do credit to both monarchs. It is an interesting fact that an English traveller, named Bell, accompanied the mission sent by the former to the latter in 1719. It may be said that broadly the relations of the two countries continued to be friendly until the period of general aggression by foreign powers, although they were on the verge of war in 1881 over disputes as to concessions in Manchuria.

In 1685 K'ang Hsi issued an edict opening all the ports of China to foreign trade, but this permission only lasted until 1757, after which date Canton alone was open to such trade. The interval saw a considerable development of trade in the South. Prior to this, England had made several efforts to develop trade relations with China, mainly through the East India Company, which established a factory at Amoy and another at Canton. The first attempt seems to have been an expedition which went out with a letter from Queen Elizabeth to the Emperor in 1596. The ship was wrecked and all hands were lost. It was, however, in the reign of Ch'ien Lung (the other really great Manchu Emperor, 1735–1795) that Britain succeeded in presenting her demands at Peking. The famous embassy from George III to Ch'ien Lung, under the leadership of Lord Macartney, received a courteous hearing, but the Emperor again took the view that the presents brought by the mission were of the nature of tribute. The proposals brought by Lord Macartney were for the appointment of a British trade representative at Peking, and for facilities for trading at certain Chinese ports which were at that time closed. The reply has been preserved, and is a masterpiece of dignity and firmness. One by one the requests are dealt with, and George III is addressed as though he were an ignorant child to be quietly shown his errors and presumption. After arguing that an embassy in Peking would serve no useful purpose in regard to trade, the reply continues :—

"If you assert that your reverence for our Celestial dynasty fills you with a desire to acquire our civilization—our ceremonies and laws differ so completely from your own that, even if your envoy were able to acquire the rudiments of our civilization, you could not possibly transport our manners and customs to your alien soil. Therefore, however adept the envoy might become, nothing would be gained thereby. . . . As your ambassador can see for himself, we possess all things. I set no value on objects strange or ingenious, and have no use for your country's manufactures. This, then, is my answer to your request to appoint a representative at my court, a request contrary to our dynastic usage which would only result in inconvenience to

EARLY INTERNATIONAL CONNECTIONS 53

yourself. I have expounded my wishes in detail and have commanded your tribute envoys to leave in peace on their homeward journey. It behoves you, O King, to respect my sentiments and to display even greater devotion and loyalty in future, so that by perpetual submission to one throne, you may secure peace and prosperity for your country hereafter."

In a second message the Emperor makes excuses for King George's ignorance. " I do not forget," he says, " the lonely remoteness of your island, cut off from the world by intervening wastes of sea, nor do I overlook your excusable ignorance of the usages of our Celestial Empire. I have consequently commanded my ministers to enlighten your ambassador on the subject, and have ordered the departure of the mission."[1]

Bertrand Russell, after quoting parts of this reply, says with some truth, " What I want to suggest is that no one understands China until this document has ceased to seem absurd."[2] A Chinese historian, however, commenting on the incident, says, " it had a good deal to do with the natural vanity of China. It confirmed the belief of the Chinese scholars that their Emperor was the universal sovereign. For this self-conceit China has paid dearly ever since."[3]

This brings us down to the early part of last century, and the beginning of a period of conflict between China and the Western Powers. Before attempting to trace this recent history and to show its bearings on the present position, let me attempt to draw a few general conclusions from the long and curious history we have glanced at in this chapter.

---

[1] See *Annals of Memoirs of the Court of Peking*, pp. 320 ff.
[2] *The Problem of China*, p. 51.
[3] *Outlines of Chinese History*, p. 464.

The relations of China with other peoples seem to have been mainly along three lines—religious, military and commercial. In the matter of religion and culture China has shown herself tolerant, with a few exceptions, willing to receive new ideas and able to assimilate them. Having a well-thought-out system of her own, she has not been easily turned from her own way, and even Buddhism, which had more influence on Chinese life than any other outside religion, took many centuries to gain a really firm hold and was deeply modified in the process. Only once or twice, so far as I know, was there anything that could be called persecution, though there was strong opposition at other periods.

In the matter of war China has not always been able to resist outside aggression. She has never, under her own rulers, been really aggressive.[1] During the Mongol and Manchu dynasties alone have there been any considerable attempts at foreign conquests. The interesting thing is that China has been very little influenced in her inner life and in her social structure by these military invasions, or by the dominance of foreign rulers. Her own inner strength is scarcely to be seen anywhere more clearly than in the way in which she has conquered. her conquerors.

In the matter of commerce, up to the period we have now reached, there is not much to say. China did not in the main seek foreign commerce; it was thrust upon her. She has not been altogether unwilling to trade with other nations, but during these many centuries she evidently felt that little was to be gained by such trade. The effect of attempting to force foreign trade upon China without any real understanding of her customs and methods

[1] The conquests of the T'angs were mainly by way of consolidating kindred peoples.

EARLY INTERNATIONAL CONNECTIONS 55

had, even before 1840, produced a good deal of resentment and friction. We shall see in the next chapter how this has developed, and how these three methods of intercourse have become mingled and inter-related, while the whole process has been immeasurably accelerated.

CHAPTER IV

COMING INTO THE FAMILY (1840-1911)

We have now to turn our attention to the processes by which China has been drawn into close relations with the other nations of the world. It is a long and not a very edifying story reflecting little credit on any of the parties concerned. It is clearly impossible to trace it in detail. It will not, however, be difficult to give the broad outline, and see some of the main currents that are sweeping China not merely out of the eddy in which she had rocked with comparative safety for generations, but into the mid-stream of events where many forces contend, as it were, for her very life.

We have already seen how China's relations with other nations could be classified as the religious and cultural, the military and the economic. Although these three lines intersected in the long years prior to 1840, one can fairly easily disentangle them. In the period we now consider they become inextricably interwoven. Nevertheless, as a determinant of outward events, the economic is unquestionably the most important. As we proceed, however, we shall see the immense importance of the religious and cultural aspect of China's relationship with the West. Possibly to most people it is the third military aspect which is most prominently in mind when they think about the future relations of East and West. This is due to an unfortunate idea that

COMING INTO THE FAMILY (1840–1911) 57

the East is a potential menace to the West, and must be viewed in that light.

We have seen that China did not want our trade. This was due in the first place to a deep-seated conviction that foreign imports must mean the export of silver, and therefore the impoverishment of the country. While China is a very large user of silver, and has been for many generations, she never has produced any large quantity. Apparently Chinese economists had no confidence that China could produce, in silk, tea or other produce, enough to provide exchange with any large influx of foreign goods, and indeed the increase of foreign trade has induced one or two silver famines in China. Nevertheless, China's own production has been immensely stimulated by intercourse with other nations, and fears about the export of silver have not, on the whole, been realized.

Another more important element in the situation was China's sense of self-sufficiency and superiority. She had to learn some very bitter lessons before she was willing to treat with other States on equal terms. We saw how presents sent from abroad were accepted as tribute; when Lord Macartney's mission travelled to Tientsin, a Chinese flag was flying upon the vessel that conveyed him with the inscription, "A tribute bearer from the country of England."

But China had some truer reasons to fear the foreigner. The early intercourse in the South was marked by cruelty and high-handedness, and the representatives of foreign nations had shown a marked ignorance of Chinese customs and thought. It was this failure in mutual understanding which, more than anything else, precipitated the first war with Britain in 1840–42.

The story of this war and the succeeding one in

1856–60 has often been written, and there is no need to retell it in detail. One may note, in passing, that while the wars have been called the opium wars, and while the importation of opium was legalized by the treaty that concluded the second one, the issue was really a much wider one. With the elements in the situation a clash on some point was inevitable sooner or later. Opium was, indeed, the principal, though not the only article being imported by the British merchants. It was excluded by China not simply on moral and social grounds, but also because of their conviction that its import was exhausting the silver of the country, and, as a matter of fact, the local merchants and officials had for years been winking at the trade and making large profits from it. On the other hand, the Peking Government appointed, in Commissioner Liu, a man who was genuinely alarmed by the trade and determined to do all in his power to stop it for the sake of his countrymen. The British authorities determined to defend a traffic which, after many days, the House of Commons declared to be morally indefensible. They only surrendered the 20,000 cases of opium because they had no force adequate to resist the demand. Although, technically, this seizure was not the *casus belli*, there can be no doubt that it had a very large share among the several factors that ended in open rupture. While the matter was being referred to London for action a relatively trivial incident precipitated the crisis, a Chinese having been killed in a drunken brawl by some British sailors, and the British Consul refusing to hand over the culprit to the Chinese law courts.

The inwardness of the struggle is seen when we think of the wide gulf which separated a government inspired by conservatism, prejudice and pride on

COMING INTO THE FAMILY (1840–1911)   59

the one hand, and on the other the representatives of a nation trading in all parts of the world, proud also of its position and achievements, and intolerant of what seemed like needless and stupid limitations to trade. England's demand was to be treated on equal terms; China saw no reason to comply with such an outlandish request. If the opium chests had not been destroyed, and if the Chinese had not been murdered, can anyone think that a war would have been averted? The fuel was piled up and ready for the spark.

The Treaty of Nanking, which concluded the first war, established extra-territorial rights, provided for the opening of five Chinese ports to foreign trade (Canton, Amoy, Foochow, Ningpo and Shanghai), for the cession of Hong Kong to Great Britain, and for a large indemnity covering the value of the opium destroyed and the losses suffered by British subjects. It did not settle the question of the legality of the opium traffic.

It was said by the first British envoy to Peking that "in a country like China the conclusion of a treaty is the commencement, not the termination, of difficulties,"[1] and there is, unfortunately, too much truth in the aphorism. While the treaty led to free trade not only with Britain, but with other foreign nations, who shortly concluded similar treaties, it also led to many new difficulties, more particularly as the Chinese felt, naturally enough, that a treaty exacted at the point of the sword lacked any moral sanction.

In 1843, unfortunately, affairs were complicated by the intersection of our first line, namely, the religious. Three missionaries were attacked by a crowd near Shanghai and nearly lost their lives.

[1] *Recent Events and Present Policies in China*, J. O. P. Bland, p. 257.

Reparation was demanded and refused, and naval action was taken by blockading the harbour and so preventing the tribute of rice from going to Peking. This was but one of a number of incidents where difficulties arose through the meeting of people who did not understand one another.

It was in a much deeper way that the religious and cultural element entered into the situation in 1850. This year saw the beginning of the famous Taiping rebellion,[1] one of the chief causes of which was the meeting there of two alien civilizations. In its early stages it was semi-Christian; the leaders destroyed idols and temples with the utmost zeal and gathered themselves into an association for the worship of the Almighty (Shangti hwei). Very soon the ideals were lost and the nature of the rising completely changed. The Taipings took " the extermination of the Manchus " for their watchword. The leaders became demoralized by their early success and showed no constructive statesmanship. The country-side for hundreds of miles was destroyed, and half China was threatened with disorder and bloodshed. With few exceptions the generals were bandit chiefs, but it was by no means an easy thing to overcome them. As everyone knows, China turned to the despised foreigners for help, and finally, after fourteen years of strife, Gordon struck the blow which brought the insurrection to a close. Its importance from our point of view is to show one way in which new ideas coming from without began to affect Chinese life. No doubt many elements of unrest were already present and possibly some kind of rebellion might have broken out without any outside influence. The vast majority of those who took part in it were quite ignorant of Christianity

[1] So called because the original idea was that the Tai ping tien kuo (Heavenly Kingdom of Peace) was to be founded.

COMING INTO THE FAMILY (1840-1911) 61

or of the idea which had affected the pioneers of the movement. But it was these things which acted as the spark. Similar ideas have acted in different ways in the years that followed.

It was while the Taiping rebellion was still in progress that the second war with Britain was fought. In this war the French were also involved. It was another case of the clashing of two opposite ideas of what should be the relation between China and other States. The war was carried to the North—Tientsin was occupied, and a treaty was there drawn up by which China was to pay an indemnity of Tls. 4,000,000, foreigners were to be allowed to reside in Peking, and Christianity was to be tolerated. Trouble arose, however, in regard to the ratification of this treaty and the similar one with France, owing to the refusal of the Emperor to permit the envoys to come to Peking (except by the route used by tribute-bearing expeditions), as agreed when the treaty was drawn up. Hostilities broke out again, and this time were carried to Peking, Envoys under a flag of truce were captured by the Chinese and tortured. The Emperor fled from the city as the foreign forces arrived, and the troops then sacked and destroyed the summer palace outside Peking.[1] This act of vandalism was justified by its perpetrators on the ground that it was the only way of touching the Emperor himself, and no doubt it was to be preferred to pillaging towns and villages, or the slaughter of the common people in a further battle. The palace had been constructed largely under Jesuit influence and contained innumerable objects of art. Its destruction is still remembered against France and England as a terrible

[1] This was, of course, the old summer palace, in a different place from the new one built by the late Empress-Dowager with money raised for building a navy.

62 CHINA IN THE FAMILY OF NATIONS

offence, and is one of the many ways in which Western nations have trampled upon Chinese susceptibilities. Of course, the Chinese were greatly to blame for their treatment of the peace envoys and for going back on their promises, but one cannot help feeling that more patience and a deeper knowledge of Chinese character might have led to a different course of action.

To the lasting shame of England the treaty which concluded this war in 1858 legalized the opium traffic. A British minister was appointed to Peking, and more treaty ports were opened. In the Chinese version of the French treaty a clause appears giving Catholic missionaries a right to own property in the interior. It is said that this clause was introduced surreptitiously. Upon it was based for many years the claims of all missionaries to own such property. Only recently has the position been regularized.

Thus between 1840 and 1858 China was literally forced open by the sword, the chief agent being Britain and the chief motive commercial gain. It may be argued that it was for the good of China herself that she should be brought into relation with other nations, that her rulers were arrogant and ignorant to a degree, and that along with trade have come also the blessings of education, healing, and the preaching of the Gospel. Such arguments do not really touch the question. If China did not want the West, what right had the West to force an entrance ? The people of China were in no sense whatever a menace to the rest of the world. History seems to show that in course of time, if patience had been exercised, they would have been ready enough to consider new ideas brought to them in a friendly way. The method of approach was calculated to sow in the Chinese mind a sense of deep resentment and prejudice, to stiffen her antiforeign feeling and to awaken movements that might at any time lead to reprisals. When we read of such movements, let us make an effort to put ourselves in the place of the Chinese, the mass of her people relatively ignorant of foreigners, holding strongly to their own ideas and customs, awakened rudely and even cruelly at times from a peaceful slumber which they regarded as their birthright. The wonder is not that there have been " incidents " when foreigners have suffered: the wonder is that there have not been many more.

On such incidents there is no need to dwell. A massacre of Roman Catholic missionaries in Tientsin in 1870, the murder of Mr. Margary of the British Consular Service in 1874, the massacre of French priests in Annam, the murder of German missionaries in Shantung in 1897, and finally the Boxer outbreak in 1900—these are but a few of many cases where attacks by Chinese upon foreigners led to reprisals in which some fresh hold was gained upon China or her dependencies. In most cases there was blame upon both sides: in all cases we must remember that China was not primarily the aggressor, and that whether by merchant, traveller or missionary, she was being entered against her will, or at least without her active concurrence. Yet, when the outbreak took place, attention was focussed on that side of the picture which emphasized the faults of China or her subjects, and not on the extenuating circumstances or on the long previous history which had been the predisposing cause of the trouble. If the Western Powers boasted a higher civilization and a truer faith, it should have been theirs to show courtesy, forbearance, and forgiveness, and to be ready to win their way by the service they could render, rather than to drive their way in by continual aggression, and to secure indemnities and concessions by the threat or the use of military force. But all the long story of the political and commercial approach of Christendom to China shows very little that can be said to express the Spirit of Christ. China has good reason to know that there is no Christian nation, a sentiment which I found greeted with tumultuous applause when I uttered it the other day to a large audience of Chinese Christians.

The war between China and France in 1884–5 is another example of mutual misunderstandings and deception. One result was the permanent establishment of the French in Tongking. It led to some reorganization of the Chinese navy under British guidance, an instance of the way in which the "friendliness" of a foreign Power was only less serious for China than her enmity. It is one of the strange paradoxes of the meeting of East and West that the latter, after conquering the former, should devote herself to making it harder to do it next time. The Western trained troops are those which offer the strongest resistance to troops from the West. Japan's German-drilled army destroyed the German power in Shantung in 1914. At the same time it is to be noted that, so far as China was concerned, a good deal of the ammunition and other war material supplied by the West was not first-rate, and some even absolutely worthless. This was due both to the dishonesty of Western traders and the ignorance or connivance of Chinese officials who were often ready to sell their country's interest for private gain.

During this period, China's main dependencies came under foreign control ; S. Burmah and Cochin China (1862), Liu Kiu Islands and Western Ili (1881), Tongking, Annam and N. Burmah (1886), Sikkim (1890), Korea, Formosa and the Pescadores (1895).

COMING INTO THE FAMILY (1840–1911)

Passing by, for a moment, the crucial developments in Korea and Manchuria, let us bring our summary of Western intercourse with China down to 1904, when the whole situation was altered by the outbreak of the Russo-Japanese War. The collapse of China in the war with Japan marked the complete failure of the old order. From the great days of Chien Lung the Manchu power had steadily declined. The period when China had most need of wise and disinterested statesmanship to guide her in new and exceedingly intricate relationships coincided with a famine of first-rate leadership. One or two individuals showed above the mass, but there was no succession of men who could look ahead, who could see the deeper meaning of what was happening and who could grasp the situation and carry through a consistent policy. In this respect we have a marked contrast between China and Japan. In the latter country the old feudal system had been preserved. There were certain clan leaders, trained to think politically, and these men showed a wisdom, a self-restraint and a patriotism that were markedly lacking in China while she was facing a similar situation. The problem of China was indeed a much harder one, but no one can say what the present position would be if China had been able to call upon even a few first-rate statesmen in her hour of need. Even that great figure, Li Hung Chang, and his more scholarly though less astute contemporary, Chang Chih Tung, were not big enough for the situation. Li showed a skill in diplomacy that on several occasions saved China from greater humiliation. Chang saw clearly that only by boldly welcoming the new knowledge could China be saved from disaster. But the former never seems to have grasped the full significance of what was happening to his country, and the latter failed to make his influence felt in the national policy, though doing much for the provinces under his control, and in the period of reaction he lost his nerve and backed up the Empress. Both were, I believe, high-minded and patriotic men, ready to make a bridge between the old and the new, but too old and too set in their own ways to be able either to see how wide was the gulf or to take the courageous steps that alone could have saved the situation.

In November, 1897, two German missionaries were murdered in the Province of Shantung. Germany had recently awakened to what was happening in the Far East. France, England, America, Russia, had been gaining commercial and political advantage in China, while Germany had been consolidating her own Empire and resources, and concentrating on problems nearer at hand. Now, with a new sense of a world-destiny, she saw her chance of following in the wake of France and Britain and Russia. She made her moves less skilfully and perhaps a little more brutally. Substantially her policy was the same—to use China's weakness and any incident that presented a favourable opportunity as a means for securing political and commercial advantage at China's expense. China was impotent to resist. She had already learned, in wars with other Powers, how useless it was to try the issue in battle against well-equipped modern armies. She yielded rights in Shantung for mining and railways, and gave to Germany a ninety-nine years lease of Kiaochow, a port which German authorities regarded as capable of great development.

Immediately, other nations took their cue from Germany. It would be absurd to suppose that so valuable a grant to one could be allowed unless others shared the spoil. Russia demanded and received Port Arthur, Britain Wei Hai Wei, France

COMING INTO THE FAMILY (1840–1911)

Kuang Chow Wan. China was parcelled out into "spheres of influence," where different countries could exploit without interference from others. France was to have the Southern provinces (Yunnan and Kuangsi), Japan was to have Fukien, Great Britain the Yangtse Valley, Russia Manchuria. A Belgian syndicate came in to build a railway from Peking to Hankow. Italy, a little later, made a similar demand; but even the patience of the Chinese comes to an end sometime, and she was actually refused!

At this period it seemed as if China was simply like a carcase being cut up and distributed among a pack of hungry wolves. It was generally expected that, in course of time, military occupation would follow commercial exploitation. The Chinese were indignant and exasperated. They saw that their country had been "caught napping." Under a conservative and narrow-minded Empress of a foreign race they seemed powerless to meet the situation. Many of the younger men felt that, given time and non-interference, China could adapt herself to modern conditions. But these were just the elements that were lacking. The tide rushed in with tumultuous haste, and just as one position was being prepared, it was found already to be surrounded by the incoming flood. The feeling was one of deep resentment and dull despair, accentuated by the consciousness that China's own inner weakness was in part responsible for the catastrophe.

Three things happened that served to alter the situation. The first move came from America, who, having recently entered the Far Eastern world as a political force through the capture of the Philippines, declared for the policy of the open-door, and Great Britain pledged her full support. The other Powers were shamed into agreeing in a half-hearted way. This checked, for a while at any rate, the policy of "spheres of influence," and gave China some hope that the development might be a peaceful economic penetration rather than a military and political scramble.

The second event was the Boxer outbreak, and the third was the Russo-Japanese War. We must now look at these two more closely.

While, as I have said, the Chino-Japanese War gave an impetus to the aggressive designs of the Western Powers, it also aroused many Chinese to the need for more far-reaching reforms. The object lesson of a nation long regarded as almost beneath the contempt of China, a mere island in the Eastern seas, suddenly arising in her might and striking China to the dust, was one which could not be overlooked. The Emperor, stimulated by Chang Chih Tung's famous book, *Learn* (translated under the title *China's Only Hope*), proclaimed an era of reform and modern education. For a brief period he stood out before the people as the leader of the country into a new world where something more than the glories of Yao and Shun might be realized. Young China found in him her champion, and eyes turned eagerly to the future rather than to the past. Among the Imperial edicts which fell like autumn leaves upon the astonished people, were those calling for a complete change in the old examination system, for the establishment of colleges and technical schools on Western lines, for the right of direct approach to the throne, for a thorough reorganization of the government, for a remodelling of the army. Two young Cantonese were high in the councils of the young Emperor, Kang Yu Wei and Liang Chi Ch'ao. For just one hundred days the curtain seemed to lift and the nation was filled by a strange mixture of elated

COMING INTO THE FAMILY (1840–1911)

expectancy and gloomy foreboding. In the last of this series of edicts we read words that show how long a journey it was from Ch'ien Lung to Kuang Hsü. He says :—

"In promoting reforms, we have adopted certain European methods, because, while China and Europe are both alike in holding that the first object of good government should be the welfare of the people, Europe has travelled further on this road than we have, so that by introduction of European methods we simply make good China's deficiencies. But our statesmen and scholars are so ignorant of what lies beyond our borders that they look upon Europe as possessing no civilization. They are all unaware of those numerous branches of Western knowledge whose object is to enlighten the minds and increase the material prosperity of the people."

Unfortunately the enthusiasm of the Emperor and his advisers had not reckoned with two facts—the innate conservatism of the people, and the personal power and resourcefulness of the Empress-Dowager Tzü Hsi. Lulled to sleep by her apparent inaction, the Emperor allowed to slip by the crucial moment when her intrigues might have been stopped. With the cunning of a tiger she awaited her time and sprang upon her prey. In Yuan Shih Kai she found one who had been trusted by the Emperor, but was willing to turn against him. The Emperor was spared but shut up where he could do no more harm. The hundred-day reforms were cancelled. The door was, as it were, slammed in the face of the insistent West, and the first step was taken on the path that led to the Boxer outbreak, with its fateful consequences.

Naturally our sympathies go out to the young Emperor, eager to help his people and fulfil his high functions, filled with enthusiasm, and no longer bound by the pride and prejudice that had marked the rulers of China for so long. But we must remember that he was clearly before his time, that he had tried to force the pace more than an ancient people, bound by traditions, could really stand, and that he suffered, as many another would-be reformer, because he lacked the strength of character, without which such a reform movement could not be carried through against terrific obstruction and the dense ignorance of the people. He always remembered against Yuan Shi Kai the fact that his treachery had precipitated the crisis It was the memory of this betrayal that kept the South from giving their full confidence to Yuan when he took over the reigns of government as President of the Republic in 1912.

From the deposition and imprisonment of the Emperor the tide of reaction set in without any check. The Boxer movement was the expression of this among the common people. China has always been a land of secret societies, and their influence has generally been a baneful one. This movement, as everyone knows, did irreparable damage not only to the cause of missions and Christianity, but to China herself. It was the culminating point in the reactionary movement, and the Empress encouraged it, secretly at first and then publicly. Finally, when she saw that it was doomed to failure, she embarked upon an elaborate policy of hedging. All along she had apparently been in two moods, torn between her violent dislike of foreigners on the one hand, and on the other hand her sense of the realities of the situation which warned her, against her wishes and passion, that she was backing the wrong horse. The Boxer uprising was only put down after the advance of the Allied troops to Peking, where again Western civilization was

COMING INTO THE FAMILY (1840–1911)

disgraced in the eyes of China by the sack of the Imperial Palace, the destruction and theft of many priceless treasures, and the lack generally of respect for much that China reverenced. In Peking peace was dictated after many months of negotiation. Besides providing for the punishment of a number of high officials (though not, of course, of the chief offender, the Empress-Dowager) the treaty secured a final adjustment on the vexed question of the reception of foreign ministers by the Emperor, and arranged for the payment of a huge indemnity of 450 million taels, to be paid in annual instalments spread over forty years.

The Boxer outbreak had several very notable effects. It gave Western nations an indication that all was not well in their relations with China. They were not dealing simply with an effete government which could be bullied or bribed into accepting any demands, however outrageous. In China there was a deep substratum of resentment towards foreign aggression. No doubt most Westerners still put it all down to the prejudice and stupidity of a semi-civilized people. But there must have been a good many whose eyes were opened by this terrible reaction to the fact that there were deep-seated causes for the dislike of the foreigner. I am interested in seeing how even so blatant a Westerner as Mr. Bland in *China under the Empress-Dowager* pauses for a moment in his narrative to point out that all Chinese and Manchu officials (the book was written before the days of the Republic) " agree and unite in frankly confessing to their hatred of the foreigner and all his wishes. Those," he says, " who pose as the friends of foreigners merely advocate dissimulation as a matter of expediency. The thought should . . . lead us to consider what are the causes, in us or in them, which produce so constant and so deep a hatred."[1] Without necessarily endorsing the statement, one may admit that it is near enough to the truth to make us ask some very heart-searching questions. Backhouse and Bland do not pursue the subject beyond suggesting that it may be due to fear for their craft. We shall, perhaps, after the story reviewed in these pages, be able to reach a conclusion reflecting less credit on ourselves and the countries to which we belong!

But the Boxer outbreak had also a very important internal result. It showed China that it was really no use to try to throw off Western influence and revert to the "good old days." For good or ill the West had gained too great a hold on China to be simply driven away in a fit of fury. That was not the solution of the problem. A few great Chinese saw this before 1900, notably the two officials Yüan Ch'ang and Hsü Ching Ch'eng who lost their lives for protesting against Tzü Hsi's policy of encouraging the Boxers, and the Viceroys who withheld the decrees she sent out ordering the extermination of all foreigners. After the siege of Peking, with all the further indignities that she suffered, China as a whole may be said to have learnt the lesson, far as many were from being reconciled in spirit to the inevitable. Very soon the Empress was re-enacting the same reforms for which the Emperor had suffered, though she did it more cautiously. Reactionary China had learnt in a very bitter experience that she could not live to herself. She had been forced to accept her position as a member of the world family. Looking back, one can certainly say that the process was needlessly severe, that little, if any, heed was paid to her susceptibilities, and we may even doubt whether China has gained anything commensurate with what she has lost.

[1] Op. cit., p. 334.

But we cannot help admitting that the process was inevitable, that forces were at work which were certain, sooner or later, to bring her into the family, and that blame for the suffering entailed in the process cannot all be laid at the door of the Western nations.

The third event which served to check the exploitation of China by Western nations was the Russo-Japanese War. In order to understand this we must go back to an earlier point in history. While most of the European Powers were jostling one another in China proper, each jealous lest the other should steal a march upon her, Russia was quietly consolidating her position and tightening her grip upon the area north of the Great Wall. It is unnecessary to trace all the steps that led to the treaty in 1881, by which for a short time the Russian advance was checked. She was engaged in the steady, persistent search for an ice-free port, but she was anxious to maintain friendly relations with China, or at any rate to avoid open war. In the following year Korea was opened to intercourse with the West. This was the result of the Japanese advance in that country and the forcible opening of certain ports to Japanese trade. Already at that date Japan was beginning to learn lessons from European methods in China, and she was trying experiments on a small scale in Korea. This country was nominally a vassal state to China, and it was a matter of some importance to China, for the defence of her own frontiers, that Korea should not come under the control of any foreign power. Russia, on the one hand, and Japan, on the other, looked to Korea as fair game. Each took every possible opportunity for increasing its hold. The unsettled state of Korea in 1894 led to a request from the King for troops from China. The fact that these were sent without notice being first given to Japan [1] was made an excuse by the latter Power for pouring in an army of her own, and very soon the two countries were at war. China was out-manœuvred at sea and out-generalled on land. Her reorganized fleet and army proved quite unable to stand up to the Japanese, although in one or two battles a desperate resistance was offered. The treaty which concluded the war gave Korea nominal independence, and ceded the Liaotung Peninsula (with Port Arthur), the Pescadores and Formosa to Japan. Russia, Germany and France united, by threat of war, to deprive Japan of what she regarded as one of the main fruits of her victory, namely, the Liaotung Peninsula, in place of which she was compelled to accept a further large indemnity. As a reward for befriending China, Russia was given permission to carry the Trans-Siberian Railway through Manchuria to Vladivostok and to build branch lines to Moukden and Port Arthur. Thus were sown the seeds of the Russo-Japanese War, some ten years later.

A glance at the map will show the nature of the problem that lay behind this encounter. Three parties laid claim to Korea. By national affinities and by tradition China was the state which should have controlled Korean affairs, if that country were unable to control her own. China, however, was unable to deal with her own problems, and was manifestly unable to help Korea in any effective way. The Korean Government was weak and corrupt. Russia from the north-west was extending her vast domains and obviously desired to engulf Korea. She obtained large timber and other concessions, and it was clear to Japanese statesmen that unless

---

[1] A previous treaty between China and Japan provided that such notice should be given.

COMING INTO THE FAMILY (1840–1911)

she was checked she would soon be in complete control and able to threaten the shores of Japan. While Japan could afford to see Korea independent, even if weak and ill-governed, she did not feel able to look with equanimity upon so near a neighbour under the power of what then was one of the great European Imperial systems. It is easy to blame Japan for her Korean policy, and there are aspects of it which no one can excuse. But we must understand the nature of her dilemma. A weak Korea meant a Korea dominated by Russia. There was not the smallest chance of either China or Korea effectively resisting such a domination. Japan's only hope of salvation seemed to be to stop Russia before it was too late and to maintain her own position in Korea so strongly as to obviate the danger of a Russified neighbour across the Straits of Tsushima. Even if Japan had not had an imperialistic policy, and had not desired to gain the immense economic advantage which would accrue through the exploitation of Korea and perhaps of Manchuria, the policy of self-defence in a world of predatory states marked out her course in this affair. She chose her time with skill. She struck quickly and hard and repeatedly. When almost exhausted financially, and well knowing that prolongation of the war would change the situation to her loss, she let it be known that she would listen to overtures of peace from a neutral state. By appearing to insist upon demands unacceptable to Russia and in the end withdrawing them, Japan obtained a treaty which gave her all that she really wanted. Russia recognized Japan's paramount influence in Korea; she transferred to Japan the lease of the Liaotung Peninsula, ceded half the island of Saghalien, and handed over the control of the Chinese Eastern Railway from the coast to Kwanchengtze.

76 CHINA IN THE FAMILY OF NATIONS

The effects of the Russo-Japanese War have been immense in China and in regard to China's destiny. I may summarize these effects as follows :—

1. At first there was a sense of relief and gratitude in China because the menace of Russia had been destroyed. Japan was the champion of the East against the West. I was in Tientsin when the Russian fleet was being sunk a few hundred miles away in the Straits, and I can well remember with what satisfaction the news was received by the Chinese.

2. This led to a great turning towards Japan. What she had done China could do. Tens of thousands of Chinese students flocked to the Japanese Universities. Missions were sent further afield to discover the secrets that Japan had so skilfully learnt from the West.

3. It was not long, however, before China discovered that Japan was going to throw away her priceless opportunity of befriending her weaker brother. Chinese students were treated with indignity in Japan. The policy of the country was to exploit rather than to help her neighbour. Russia had been effectively checked, if not finally defeated, and Western nations realized at last that a force had arisen in the East which could challenge and even outdo them in the policy of grab. But if the yoke of Russia in the North had been heavy, that of Japan was yet more so. China discovered that she had fallen out of the frying-pan into the fire.

4. The stimulus to reform, however, remained. The people of China had already been made aware of the impotence of their old methods to meet the new situation. There was a general determination to discover the real secrets of adjusting the country in the light of modern knowledge. Not along the lines of Japanese development could China proceed to remodel her government. She must go further

back to the source from which Japan had drawn her inspiration and apply the new knowledge in her own way to meet her own quite different needs. Increasingly since the close of the Russo-Japanese War has China turned rather to America than to Japan to find the inspiration and help she needs.

CHAPTER V

THE REPUBLIC OF CHINA

PRESIDENTS OF THE CHINESE REPUBLIC.
Sun Yat Sen . . . . 1911–12 (2 months)
Yuan Shih Kai . . . 1912–15
    (Emperor for a few weeks)
Li Yuen Hung . . . 1915–17
    (Manchu restoration abortive)
Feng Kuo Chang . . . 1917–18
Hsü Shih Ch'ang . . . 1918–22
Li Yuen Hung (second term) . 1922

SOUTHERN REPUBLIC.
Sun Yat Sen 1920–22

WE have brought our record of China's relations to the foreign states down to the close of the Russo-Japanese War and we have noted how that war affected the Chinese situation. We can now turn aside from this political, military and commercial interchange between China and the West and consider the internal political changes in large measure a result of influences from without.

Never in history has it proved to be an easy thing for a nation radically to alter her form of government. Often such changes have been accompanied by much bloodshed, by a longer or shorter period of unsettlement or anarchy, and by the creation or deepening of bitter feuds between different sections of the people. China's change from autocracy to democracy is no exception, save only that in the matter of bloodshed and violence her record up to the present is probably a good deal

THE REPUBLIC OF CHINA

better than that of most of the Western examples that suggest themselves.

While the central government of China up to 1911 had always been of the autocratic type, it must be remembered that there were certain directions in which the country had been prepared for the introduction of democratic institutions. These may be summarized in the following points :—

1. Philosophically the right of the people to rebel had, as we have seen, been maintained by Mencius. The Emperor was regarded as a trustee responsible, in the last resort, to the people. If he betrayed the trust the people had the remedy in their own hands.

2. Again and again—some twenty-four times—in Chinese history the people had actually used that remedy. The Emperor could see for himself, by consulting the records, that the Chinese democracy was a fact with which to reckon.

3. The system of selecting advisers, legislators and minor officials which came down from the Ch'in dynasty was that the headman of each locality recommended scholars of distinction to the throne. Through these men the Emperor could keep in touch with the wishes of his people in every part of his domain. When this was altered to the examination system during the Tsin dynasty (sixth century A.D.) it was supposed that this would give an even better chance for men of merit—however lowly their origin—to share in the government. The nature of the examination and the long and expensive preparation required largely neutralized this idea, but even under this system there have been many examples of officials springing from humble homes.

4. Even more important is the fact that a large amount of local self-government had been developed throughout the country. Within each family

you have a miniature kingdom, the family often consisting of a large number of persons. The heads of the families or clans in any village or market-town constitute an informal group for carrying on certain public services, arbitrating in disputes, and even at times trying criminal cases. Moreover the trade laws or conventions in China are those set in operation not by the central or local government but by the trade guilds, organized on a democratic basis.[1] The local gentry, the chambers of commerce, and now the educational associations, are factors that have a very considerable influence on local and provincial government, and such organizations are far more democratic than is any central government that China had known before the Republic.

At the same time it may well be questioned whether China as a whole was at all adequately prepared for so sweeping a change as that which took place in 1911. In the light of events we may pick out certain directions in which much more preparation was needed. Yuan Shih Kai, who, though never really believing in the ideals of the reformers, was at any rate an astute observer of the life of China, gave his views in the following words: "I doubt whether the people of China are at present ripe for a Republic or whether, under present conditions, a Republic is adapted to the Chinese people. . . . The adoption of a limited monarchy would bring conditions back to the normal and would bring stability much more rapidly than that end could be attained through any experimental form of government, unsuited to the genius of the people or to the present conditions of China."[2]

[1] See Chapter IX, pp. 174–5.
[2] Quoted in *Modern China, a Political Study*, p. 16.

THE REPUBLIC OF CHINA

When we have reviewed the events of the last ten years we may be better able to judge whether this opinion has or has not been borne out by them. It may be that we are still too much in the midst of them to reach any final opinion.

Following the Russo-Japanese War the Empress-Dowager perceived that a demand by the people for a larger share in the government of the country could no longer be ignored. Shrewd enough to see what was happening, but blind enough to believe that an appearance of self-government without the real thing would keep the people quiet, the Empress promulgated a scheme for the setting up of Provincial Assemblies which were to be simply advisory bodies with no executive functions. The loudly proclaimed idea was that these bodies were to prepare the way for full representative government. Whether the Empress was sincere in this profession or not we can never certainly know, as death removed her from the scene in November 1908, long before the time came for carrying out the further changes. The Emperor Kuang Hsü had died on the previous day. The new Emperor was a child of four years old, the succession having been arranged by the Empress in order to keep the real power in her own hands. Had there been a strong and enlightened man among the Manchu princes to take the lead at this crisis it is conceivable that China might have moved by peaceful stages to a limited monarchy. Such a person was not to be found. The Regent, father to the young Emperor, and his relations were utterly unscrupulous, and had no appreciation of the real situation. Professing to carry forward the constitutional changes, they absolutely ignored the newly-created assemblies, they filled all the chief posts with Manchus, dismissing among others Yuan Shih

82 CHINA IN THE FAMILY OF NATIONS

Kai, and they sold positions in all parts of the country to the highest bidder.

Whether Yuan Shih Kai was right or not in his judgment as to China's readiness for a Republic, there is no doubt that the people were in this way prepared for a revolution. As it turned out the revolution, long anticipated by a small group of reformers, was eagerly fomented by them, and thus became not only an anti-Manchu but also a pro-Republican one. With dramatic suddenness the end came. Beginning with a protest by the people of Szechwan against the conclusion of a foreign loan for building the railway to that province, the revolt against the authorities rapidly spread down the Yangtse to Hankow and Wuchang, and involved the larger part of the south. The ground had been prepared by Sun Yat Sen, long an outlaw with a price upon his head. His agents and friends were to be found in all walks of life. The army of the south was riddled with revolutionary ideas. Li Yuen Hung, a commander in the Imperial Army at Wuchang, became the military leader. By this time the Manchus realized that they had made a mistake in dismissing the one strong man who had trained the only modern army in China. Yuan Shih Kai had been "allowed to go to his native place because of his poor state of health." He suddenly recovered, returned to Peking, took control of the army and of government, and insisted on the abdication of the Regent.

The Northern armies speedily advanced to Hankow and recaptured Hanyang. Here Yuan Shih Kai halted. He saw that the revolution could not be crushed, at any rate without terrible bloodshed. All he wanted was a strategic position from which to negotiate. He began by playing for a limited monarchy with a constitution similar to that

THE REPUBLIC OF CHINA

of Great Britain. Sun Yat Sen is no man for half measures. It was clear that on this basis an agreement was not possible. While matters were being discussed Nanking was captured by the Republicans. Yuan was compelled to shift his ground, and worked for satisfactory terms for the abdicating Emperor. These were agreed to. The last Manchu edict, issued in the name of the Empress-Dowager, widow of Kuang Hsü, a masterpiece of face-saving, contains the following sentences :—

"The majority of the whole people are in favour of a republic. . . . Such being the general inclination, Heaven's ordinance may be divined. How could I dare to disregard the wishes of the millions for the sake of the glory of one family ? . . . The territories of the Manchus, Chinese, Mongolians, Mohammedans and Thibetans shall be consolidated into a great Republic of China. The Emperor and I will retire into leisure to pass easily through the months and years and to see the consummation of wise government. This will indeed be excellent !"

The last act in the drama was the abdication of Sun Yat Sen as President in favour of Yuan Shih Kai, a step taken in the hope of thus uniting North and South, and in recognition of the fact that what China needed most was peace and unity. In his closing address to the Assembly at Nanking, Sun called upon the nation to show its devotion to democratic principles and to the peace ideal by helping to bring peace into the whole world.

The history of the ten years which have elapsed since the formation of the Republic is one of many changes, little real progress, unsettlement within and dangers from without—a history which may well give true lovers of China cause for discouragement though not for despair. When the Republic was set up, China was but starting out upon a voyage of discovery. She was like Columbus setting sail upon the voyage which was to lead to the discovery of a new world. Like him China had many storms to face, long hours of uncertainty and disappointment, hardship, and even the danger of mutiny. Those who proclaimed the Republic acted as if all were accomplished and the work was done. Far other were the facts. Yuan Shih Kai, as we have seen, never really believed in the Republic, and was not trusted by the predominant party in Parliament. He maintained, with some truth, that the agitation for a Republic had only served to teach the people that democracy meant no taxes and no government. He saw that China was in a parlous state, that she needed money and that she might, through anarchy, become more than ever a prey to Japan and Europe. The Parliamentarians, on the other hand, were determined to limit his powers in every way possible. Personally I believe that Yuan was sincerely convinced that he was acting for the good of China, although it is impossible to acquit him of personal ambition and lack of sympathy with many with whom it was necessary to work if the nnity of the country was to be maintained on any other basis than that of his personal ascendancy. He chose for advisers men he knew, rather than those who represented the various different elements in the nation. In short he simply did not know how to run a Republic, and it cannot be said that the Republican party knew much better.

Very soon things reached a climax. The clauses in the constitution defining the duties of the President could not be agreed upon when such different ideas prevailed, nor was Yuan ready to give to his opponents the right to elect his Cabinet, or even to submit to Parliament the agreement for a foreign loan, which was urgently needed to meet immediate

THE REPUBLIC OF CHINA 85

necessities. He signed the loan agreement over the heads of Parliament. The Radicals (Kuo-ming-tang) left Peking for the South. A new revolution broke out, and was suppressed by Yuan, and he became, to all intents and purposes, dictator. His autocracy, with only the show of constitutional support, continued with such success that even his shrewdness was deceived by his ambition. He engineered a demand that he should be called to restore the monarchy and himself act as Emperor. The members of the Provincial Assemblies were called together to vote on the momentous issue. They sat down each with a sheet of paper in front of him on which the ballot was to be cast. One of two characters was to be written on it. Beside the paper lay another on which the character for assent was written as a fair copy. Behind each representative stood (in one of the Provincial Assemblies, at any rate) a soldier quietly repeating the word " Assent ! " When the result of this " secret ballot " was declared it showed a united and unanimous nation ready to support the proposal! Yuan Shih Kai became Emperor of China by the choice of a loyal and united people!

This was the proverbial "last straw." The revolution broke out again and once more the country would have been rent in twain had it not been that, to quote a Chinese writer, " for this deadlock, Providence found a solution by calling Yuan Shih Kai to heaven." [1]

Li Yuen Hung, the general who led the central China revolutionary armies in 1911, became President on the death of Yuan, having previously been Vice-President, and having been elected as President by the Southern party prior to the decease of his predecessor. On his appointment he restored the

[1] S. G. Cheng, in *Modern China, a Political Study*, p. 25.

reality of representative government as far as he was able to do so. The conflict between the revolutionary majority in Parliament and the central executive, which still demanded more power than the proposed constitution gave to them, was, however, reopened, mainly because the Prime Minister, General Tuan Chi Jui, was really opposed to parliamentary methods and principles. The Prime Minister became virtual dictator in place of the President. The constitution was nearly completed in spite of all internal difficulties when once again the situation in the world outside destroyed the peace of China. The issue was as to whether or not China should declare war on Germany. At this stage I do not propose to dwell on the many factors that entered into the discussion. I must simply note that a strong difference of opinion developed at Peking, that the Prime Minister was determined to declare war in spite of the opposition of Parliament, and that the President thereupon dismissed him. This precipitated civil strife and led to the brief abortive effort to restore the Manchu dynasty. General Tuan was recalled to meet the situation and overcame the imperialists, while Li Yuen Hung resigned the presidency, feeling that he had been forced into unconstitutional action. He left his office with the reputation of a man of honour and patriotism, a sincere believer in the new régime, but not a strong enough man to handle the growing power of the militarists.

The result was a purely military régime, first under the presidency of General Feng Kuo Chang, and then under that of Hsü Shih Ch'ang, the bosom friend of Yuan Shih Kai. The semblance of parliamentary forms has been maintained, but everyone knows that there is no reality in them. "The power behind the throne" has been, from

THE REPUBLIC OF CHINA 87

that day to this, the man or men who could command the largest following of troops. First one general and then another has been in the ascendant. Sometimes there has been an uneasy balance between two or three, as no one knew who was the strongest, and none dared to try conclusions. The effective control of the central government has varied. So far as the foreign-controlled services are concerned, that is to say the customs, the post office and the salt gabelle, there has been a fair degree of control and unity, though even here revenues have been deflected by local officials who in many cases have been defiant of the Peking government. Several provinces have broken away, some more completely than others, and formed independent administrations, or come under the sway of different military governors, who have fought one another for no fixed principles, guided only by greed of gain and personal ambitions. Here and there a man more patriotic than the others has stood out for a brief spell. But in the main the people of China have suffered patiently under many masters. The outstanding exception to this was the effective interference of the people, largely at the instigation of the students, in ousting the so-called An Fu party, of which General Tuan was a leading member. This was really part of an anti-Japanese movement and had little relation to the constitutional issue. It only resulted in the replacement of one set of militarists by another. Its chief significance is that the people have again shown that they can, when really roused, bring about a change in the government of the country, even when all the power seems to rest with persons who have the control of troops and finance.

Before bringing this story quite up to date, I want to refer to one very important element in the situation, namely, the struggle between the North and the South. By this I am not merely referring to the actions which led to the formation of a Southern government in Canton in 1920 under Sun Yat Sen. I wish rather to examine the inwardness of the situation because it is in connection with this long-standing dispute between the two parts of China that we find a key to the real battle of principle, a far more important thing than the personal jealousies and factions which so largely govern the internal situation in China to-day.

We have already seen that the Empire of China began in what is now North China. This was the home of the great philosophies and of the civilization, literature and art that have spread all over China since those early days. At several times in Chinese history the country has been re-divided into sections, notably at the time of the Three Kingdoms and during the period that preceded the final establishment of Kublai Khan's Empire in 1280. This division has certain geographical and psychological causes. The Northerners have had to face constant incursions and have developed a military spirit, have sought rather to protect themselves, and have therefore learnt the art of sticking to one another, even when their rulers have been far from ideal. The Southerners, on the other hand, have developed more of the business and colonizing instincts. They have been a restless and adventurous race, excelling in initiative and in their power to assimilate new ideas. While broad generalizations are always dangerous, it is fair to say that there had developed a distinct difference between the peoples of Canton and the neighbouring parts on the one hand and those of Peking and the Northern provinces on the other. On the whole West China approximates more to

THE REPUBLIC OF CHINA

the independent progressive Southern type than to the slower and more conservative Northern type.

In recent history we have seen how the Taiping rebellion started in the South and spread to Nanking, but never took hold in the North. Southerners have been the leading spirits in the revolutionary movement in the last twenty years. The North has followed some way behind, and more or less reluctantly. No doubt for some two thousand years the unity of language and literature has been a considerable factor in holding North and South together. But as new ideas began to pour into the country the more receptive Southerners became much more deeply influenced, and it is not unlikely, in my view, that this fact will continue to operate for several generations, and that the problem of holding North and South together will tax the utmost resources of Chinese statesmanship. The chief modern fact operating in the other direction is the new spirit of patriotism stimulated as it has been so largely by foreign aggression.

Mr. Cheng quotes two utterances that put the opposing ideas in sharp contrast, and I venture to reproduce them here. The Prime Minister, Tuan, voiced the Northern policy in these words:—

"I hope to unite and pacify the country by the aid of my Northern colleagues. . . . The policy of attacking the south and the south-west is only adopted because the Government, in recent years, has exhausted its wisdom and ability in meeting parliamentary tumults and has been sick of party compromise. . . . Looking around the country, I find that only the real force of the Northern militarists can save and protect the country and enforce the law. . . . The break up of the Northern military party will be introductory to the break up of our country, and the extinction of the force of the North will be an omen of the extinction of China as an independent State."

On the other hand Dr. Wu Ting Fang thus expressed the Southern point of view :—

"Northern soldiery have been sent to Southern provinces to overawe the people with the mailed fist when it is notorious that the people distrust and fear the strange soldiers. Such stationing of troops reminds one of the procedure that conquerors adopt towards vanquished nations and subject races. Where military power is insufficient to permit this, . . . they do not hesitate to commission a man with a bloody record to lead several thousand undisciplined hordes to burn and pillage throughout the provinces, and, as if that were not enough, to let loose the local brigands for this purpose by furnishing them with arms and bribes. They know no law save their own interest. They acknowledge no authority save force. The highest institutions in the land, Constitution, Parliament, President, are nothing to them."

Whatever we may think of the sincerity of the actual speakers, it is clear that there is a case for each side, that there is a radical difference in viewpoint and that skill and forbearance are needed if any political unity is to be achieved.

It may thus be said that while most of the internal warfare since the Revolution has been due to the self-interest of individual war-lords, there has been and still is a deep difference between the conservative and the radical elements. This difference expressed itself in the establishment of the Southern Republic under the presidency of Sun Yat Sen in 1920.

The impression which I gained of this Republic and of the President himself may be of interest. I paid a visit to Canton in the autumn of 1921.

THE REPUBLIC OF CHINA

Very different opinions were current as to the Republican government. I was told on the one hand that they were a set of adventurers, that there was no stability in the government, that its reforms were paper reforms and that its authority extended scarcely at all beyond the city and its immediate surroundings. On the other hand there were those who believed it to be the one hope for China, a government which had already made a complete change in the province, and which would shortly be seen to be the one really stable and honest government for China as a whole.

Neither view seemed to me to be borne out by the facts. The city government, under the mayor, a son of the President, seemed to be efficient and progressive. Certain great abuses had been tackled with success and others were being dealt with gradually. Much rebuilding of the city was being undertaken. Broad roads were being cut right through the crowded native city, regardless of all rights of property—and even of the comfort of the citizens and their families. Houses were cut in two and no compensation offered, on the ground that the property had more than doubled in value by being brought on to a main road! Strikes had been settled in several cases by the intervention of the authorities, almost entirely in favour of the strikers (and it was reported that a day's wage of all members of the union had been more than once voted to the President as a thank-offering for his intervention). It was easy to understand that a government so strongly socialist in its tendency and not at all inclined to agree to the demands of foreign capitalists would meet with opposition and be spoken of slightingly in Hong Kong.

My own feeling was that there were a number

of high-minded men in the government, that they were sincerely convinced that they were working for the good of China, and that in several cases they had really achieved something of value. At the same time I could not feel any confidence that the government would be able to last, or that it would prove in the end a satisfactory one. The following reasons led me to these conclusions.

1. In the first place the President himself seemed to me to be a man who could not see more than one side of a question. I talked with him for a long time quite intimately. He was entirely unaffected and approachable—a democrat in manner as well as in theory. He showed a wide interest in what was happening in the world, a considerable knowledge of affairs, as for example conditions in India, and a keen sympathy with progressive movements. But I found that he scarcely seemed aware of the fact that there was another side to some questions we discussed, and was unable to appreciate that there might be a modicum of right in a point of view which was, on the whole, wrong. It seemed to me that sooner or later he was bound to fail in actually carrying out even those policies in which he was in the main right and where he had the confidence of most of the people, as was the case when I was there. His record has shown also that he has failed to choose men wisely for the various positions of trust he has had to fill, and I felt that one or two of those I met were manifestly unfit for their work. Of course the President must have had great difficulty in choosing his associates, but I am disposed to think that he had not shown great wisdom in some of his selections.

2. At the time when I was in Canton the rift between the President and Ch'en Ch'ung Ming had already begun, and it seemed to me that the same

THE REPUBLIC OF CHINA 93

difficulties, partly personal, and partly matters of principle, which had broken up the Northern government, were in danger of having a like effect in the South. At the same time it is fair to say that, as far as I could judge, there was much less graft in Canton than in Peking.

3. Perhaps the matter which gave me chief apprehension was the fact that Dr. Sun was set upon a policy of military conquest. I spoke to him very frankly on this matter and told him that such a policy, while it might add a province or two to the South, would have far less effect in unifying China than a steady period of good government in the two provinces already under his control. To establish there a régime of peace and prosperity, and to show that this part of China could be governed by Chinese, without interference from the North or from foreigners, would, I maintained, do more than anything else to convince the world that the Republic should be acknowledged, and also to bring other provinces into alliance with Kwangtung and Kwangsi, in a united states of China or other similar unity. After my talk with Sun Yat Sen I discovered that this very point was one of those at issue between himself and Ch'en Ch'ung Ming, and that the latter had refused to lead the Southern forces in the Northern expedition. It proved to be an ill-fated one, and was a chief cause leading to the collapse of Sun's administration. In short, what was happening was that the South was forsaking the very principles for which it stood and taking up the methods of the North.

4. A fourth reason that led me to doubt the possibility of permanence in the Southern government was the evident failure to maintain order in many parts of the province. It must be confessed that there was a good deal of what is called

"face-pidgin" in the affairs of that government, and that when once you forsook the beaten track very little could be seen of the boasted reforms.

It is quite true that, at that time, the government had the support of the mass of the people in Canton itself. Speaking there I found an atmosphere very different from that in the North. Instead of pessimism and a sense of the uselessness of trying to oppose a corrupt government except by the slow methods of education, I found a sense of elation and hope among the students and educated people. They believed that they were on the road towards realizing their dreams. In spite of my sympathy with a number of the specific reforms, I could not share that confidence. One thing that interested me was to find that a method of functional representation was being worked out for the municipal council, a plan which I should expect to see tried in other parts of China, as it seems to be specially suitable for that country.

To return to the situation in the North and in China generally, a fuller reference may be made to the ideas embodied in the provisional constitution. This document is even now, while I write, in process of revision and will doubtless be materially changed. But as it is almost the only document we have which can give us any clear idea of what revolutionary China is striving for in the matter of government I think it is worth some attention.

The only part of the constitution which can be regarded as permanently adopted is the section referring to the President. Even the validity of this clause would be widely challenged, as it was forced through by Yuan Shih Kai in order to regularize his own position, and was used to give him " authority " to disregard constitutional methods.

THE REPUBLIC OF CHINA 95

In any case, it is only provisionally adopted. This clause provides for the election of the President by both Houses of Parliament in joint session. His term is five years and he can be re-elected once. He is the source of all executive powers. With the exception of the Cabinet and foreign ambassadors all appointments are made by him solely. He can only declare war with the approval of Parliament and his veto on Bills can be over-ridden by a two-thirds majority in Parliament.

The Houses of Parliament are two, the upper elected mainly by nomination, the lower by representation from the provinces. In theory this body exercises all legislative functions and has complete financial control. In practice it has been scarcely at all in operation, the Cabinet having nominally exercised supreme power under the direction of presidents, premiers or war-lords. The Cabinet idea is an old one in China, the Emperors for generations having surrounded themselves with a group of councillors responsible for different departments of government. During the Manchu supremacy a military council was created, and exercised far greater power than the civil council, which became a mere ornament in the machine of State. Not until the last year of the Manchu dynasty was the military council abolished. According to the provisional constitution the Cabinet is the organ for executive functions and is responsible to Parliament. Under Yuan Shih Kai it was utterly subservient to him. Under his successor it, or the Prime Minister acting for it, became supreme, and the President had simply to accept its advice as does our King. This battle between President and Cabinet has been one of the chief issues in the recent history of China, but it must not be supposed that the Cabinet has generally fought for parliamentary

96 CHINA IN THE FAMILY OF NATIONS

supremacy. It has rather fought for its own hand as against the President. More often than not it has been the tool of one of the war-lords. It is very doubtful whether Chinese political ideas have yet developed so far as to make full parliamentary government practicable.

The chief difficulties seem to me to be lack of mutual confidence springing from lack of men of public spirit and strength of character in the higher offices, a wide-spread system of peculation which is by no means coming to an end with the establishment of a Republic, indifference of the people generally to the problems of politics, largely due to lack of education and information on public affairs, domination of the situation by a few men with large resources of money and soldiers, and last but not least, continual influence of foreign countries affecting the political situation and making steady government almost impossible. In this last connection we must mention the lack of a sound financial policy. Foreign interference in connection with the many loans required is thus almost inevitable.

To me it seems that the following lines of policy should be followed if China's internal affairs are to be straightened out : [1]

1. It is essential that in some way the civil authority should be separated from the military, and that the army should not be allowed to dominate policy. It looked as if this might be on the point of happening a few months ago when Wu Pei Fu, after military victories that put him in control of the central government, called Li Yuen Hung back to office, summoned the old Parliament and retired to Pao Ting Fu with the assurance that

[1] See also the latter half of Chapter XI, where fuller suggestions are given.

he did not wish to interfere in politics, but only to see that constitutionalism got a fair chance. Unfortunately his profession has not been followed by his practice.

2. Provincial autonomy over a very large range of subjects seems to me to be desirable. I do not think the Southern and Western provinces will come in on any unified system unless they are largely autonomous, and even if a single centralized government were desirable, with the present imperfect transport arrangements and with the long history of internal warfare, I think time would have to elapse before it could be established. In the meantime there seems to be no hope of unity without a large measure of local autonomy.

3. It is of first importance that foreign interference should be reduced to a minimum. In the present financial situation, it is hard to see how China can reorganize her national life without foreign credits, and these are not likely to be given without some form of control over certain aspects of Chinese life. But I feel this should be reduced to the minimum, and I think the greatest danger to China's peaceful development lies in the continuance of the past policy where China has been the victim of international jealousies and ambitions.

4. What I have already said will show how great is the need for education for citizenship throughout China. I do not think that this need wait for a complete system of primary and secondary education to be established, with enough school places for all the population, highly desirable as this is. There is very much to be done in adult education through lectures and special schools and literature. Much more attention needs to be given to the type of education given. A true understanding of the country's needs and her position among the nations

of the world should be given to the people generally —and I would say that very many are able to assimilate such ideas. They should be the basis of a truer patriotism and a keener political conscience. A movement similar to the Workers' Educational Association in this country would be of great value. In this task I think the Christian forces have a very important part to play, and it is a notable fact that among the younger men who are coming to take a leading and honourable part in public life, a surprisingly large proportion are the graduates of Christian institutions and in a number of cases actually Christian men. Such education should be directed both to the development of a thoughtful electorate and to the creation of leaders of character and ability. It seems to me that a modified form of the old civil-service examination system should be set up, definitely directed to discovering talent in dealing with economic, social and international questions in a broad and far-seeing way. This would seem to be in line with China's own past experience, and if carried on without graft and favouritism would be as likely as any other method to give a chance to the many young men and women of ability and public spirit who are growing up in China and are eager to serve her.

5. The speedy adoption of a constitution seems to be an urgent need. So long as there are disputes on that matter it is hard to get on with the business of State. I should advocate setting up a constitution for a definite period of, say, ten years and giving it a fair trial, but making it quite easy to revise it after such an interval. By this means China would have a chance to settle down and see how far she could adapt herself to democratic institutions. A constitution so adopted could be accepted even if not felt to be ideal because it was known to

THE REPUBLIC OF CHINA

be an experiment. At the same time the experiment should be given a fair trial by all concerned. As already stated my own view is that it should provide for a very large provincial self-government.

Perhaps it is unwise for a foreign observer to venture on such specific suggestions as the above, and I do so with deference. I see in China's present position grave cause of anxiety both for herself and for the rest of the world. The unity and the good government of China are matters of interest to all of us, for an unsettled and weak country only gives fresh opportunity for exploitation and is a constant temptation to the worst elements in other nations. It is far more likely, in my view, that a weak and distracted China will lead to war in the world than that a strong and healthy China will do so. I must leave till a later point the reasons which lead me to feel hopeful about China's future. To look at the last ten years only may well lead to disheartenment. I hope to be able before we close to give good reason for a different view. In the meantime no good comes of closing our eyes to the darker facts.

CHAPTER VI

JAPAN IN CHINA

WE must now discuss one of the most difficult of all the questions concerning China's relationships to foreign Powers. We have already seen how Japan, in conquering China, gained a hold over Korea, and how, in conquering Russia, she won a place for herself in the Far East which she steadily continued to use to her own advantage. The way in which Japan threw away her chance of helping China is one of the greater tragedies of history. She had brilliantly adapted herself to meet the entirely new world situation in the midst of which she found herself at the dawn of the Meiji Era. She had drawn her inspiration from many different quarters, and had been able to take her place among the great nations of the world as one of themselves. Some measure of adaptation there must be, if nations are to live together and work together in this complex modern world. This much Japan saw; and her Elder Statesmen, representing the great families which had come to control the country, were wide enough awake to act with vigour and promptness when the crisis came. Because in some important respects Japan copied the worse rather than the better side of European life, we have no right to blame her. She had to copy the worse side in order to save herself from exploitation and very possibly from dismember-

JAPAN IN CHINA

ment. It is very usual now to hold up Japanese imperialism and all its ways to scorn and criticism. I am no defender of this aspect of Japanese policy; but one must be fair to Japan and admit at the outset that she was driven into it by Europe, and that it was the quite obvious reaction of an alert people to the environment in which they found themselves when they emerged from their long isolation.

In an incredibly short space of time Japan equipped herself to meet the West with its own weapons. She threw her energy into the creation of a commercial system and an industrial machine that could compete with Western business houses and so build up the material basis of a new army and navy. She went to Germany to remodel the former and to England for creating the latter. She began to think in terms of economic imperialism. She saw that coal and iron were the sinews of war and must be secured on the Asiatic mainland as a supplement to her own meagre supply. She learnt that in modern warfare the only defensive that can hope for quick success is a vigorous offensive. She saw that pledges given under one set of circumstances were often broken when the circumstances changed or when the contracting power thought it safe to break them. She learned the arts of our secret diplomacy and learned them very well. She even saw that patriotism was an all-powerful asset to the political prestige of a country, and she set about the deliberate fostering of a peculiarly forceful type of patriotism, virtually manufacturing a religion and falsifying her own history in order to give it the highest possible sanction.[1] The whole course of events in Japan during the last fifty years

[1] See *The Invention of a New Religion*, by B. H. Chamberlain, and *Democracy and the Eastern Question*, by T. F. Millard, pp. 18 ff.

proves not her special moral depravity so much as her amazing power of learning the lessons which Western nations were teaching her all the time, not by their professions, but by their actions in the Far East.

I shall have some hard things to say about Japanese policy, and no good purpose is served by keeping silence about it ; but I cannot see that any European nation can cast a stone at her in regard to these matters, and even the United States can scarcely throw more than a pebble. Had Japan been Christian in a sense in which no nation is, I imagine that she might have found some other way of maintaining her self-respect and possibly her integrity as a nation. But certainly there was no historical or contemporary example to guide her in finding such a course. It is also possible that with great wisdom, patience and self-restraint she might have copied the example of the West just enough to resist aggression, but not so much as to become a menace to others. But the study of the psychology of nations makes one wonder whether this really was a possibility without some great change of heart among the people generally. These are vain speculations. The fact remains that Japan did the obvious thing for any alert and virile people. She saw she must adapt herself to meet the new situation and she did it thoroughly—relentlessly.

I have said that when Japan threw away her chance of befriending China, one of the great tragedies of history was enacted. But I do not wish by that to suggest that the Japan we see in her international policy during the last seventeen years is the Japan I should have wished to see as China's counsellor and friend. I mean rather that

Japan which could have seen that opportunity

JAPAN IN CHINA 103

would have been the Japan that might have helped China to solve her problem in a finer way than Japan has met hers. For there are two Japans, as there are two Germanys, two Englands and two Frances. Before I close this subject I must speak of the true Japan, and we must consider what hope there is of that change of heart to which I have referred. Now we must pass to a consideration of events, only cautioning ourselves against judging too harshly on the basis of these alone. I shall deal with them, for the sake of convenience, under the following heads: Korea; Shantung and the twenty-one demands; China's entry into the war; Japan's "special position" in China; financial penetration; the demoralization of China; and events subsequent to the Great War.

Korea.

I have already tried to explain why Japan, if actuated by the motives that ordinarily govern international activities, could not afford to see a weak Korea liable to be controlled by any other power. The Korean Government had become corrupt and inefficient. There did not seem to be any hope of improvement. Russia was becoming a dangerous neighbour, China was unable to handle any problems but her own. Japan's course seemed quite obvious. All this we must admit. But such a presentation of the case gives no justification for many of the incidents connected with the Japanese régime in Korea. These have been fully set forth in various books, and I do not think any good purpose will be served by repeating the details. Step by step Japan tightened her grip on Korea. She made treaties only to mark stages in the process of assimilation, abrogating one after

104 CHINA IN THE FAMILY OF NATIONS

another as opportunity offered. She got her excuses for this policy, as often as not, in some folly committed by the Korean Government or people. In fact she copied, with remarkable skill and with a more complete result, the methods which, as we have seen, European nations had used in their dealings with China and her dependencies. The nervousness shown by the Japanese Government in the notorious conspiracy case could be paralleled by the experience of other imperial powers, such as the French action in unearthing a so-called revolutionary plot in Madagascar a few years ago, and perhaps some not very distant episodes in the government of India. The methods of torture used to extract the kind of evidence the police desired are not much less inexcusable than certain events at Amritsar, though they were in themselves a terrible example of what a bureaucratic and militaristic government can do with a subject people. Wherever one goes in Korea to-day one sees the effects of this systematic and terrible repression of a people. A very deep rift has been made between Japanese and Koreans, and it is almost certain to my mind, that Korea never will be satisfied to accept Japanese rule. The non-violent demonstrations of the whole people in 1919 were an eloquent witness to this fact. As I am only referring to Korea incidentally in so far as Japan's policy there bears on the Chino-Japanese situation, I do not propose to attempt to describe even this remarkable movement. It is enough to say that it was an expression of the determination of Koreans never to acquiesce in the Japanese rule. The leaders of the movement, acting under the strong influence of Korean Christians, did their utmost to prevent violence. They issued these instructions:—

"Whatever you do, do not insult the Japanese,

do not throw stones, do not hit with your fists, for these are the acts of barbarians."

The demonstrations united men, women and children throughout the country in a proclamation of independence containing the following words :—

"We herewith proclaim the independence of Korea and the liberty of the Korean people. We tell it to the world in witness of the equality of all nations and we pass it on to our posterity as their inherent right. . . . We have no wish to find special fault with Japan's lack of fairness or her contempt for our civilization and the principles on which her state rests ; we, who have greater cause to reprimand ourselves, need not spend precious time in finding fault with others. . . .

"Our part is to influence the Japanese Government, dominated as it is by the old idea of brute force, which thinks to run counter to reason and universal law, so that it will change, act honestly and in accord with the principles of right and truth."

One can scarcely imagine a more dignified or truly Christian protest against what Koreans felt and feel to be a great moral wrong, the attempt, that is, to take away the nationality of the people and to bind on them a hateful yoke. The appeal was to the better mind of Japan, stimulated largely by President Wilson's noble utterances about the rights of smaller nations. Towards the close of the proclamation we read :—

"To-day Korean independence will mean not only daily life and happiness for us, but also it would mean Japan's departure from an evil way, and exaltation to the place of true protector of the East, so that China, too, even in her dreams, would put all fear of Japan aside. This thought comes from no minor resentment, but from a large hope for the future welfare and blessing of mankind."

106 CHINA IN THE FAMILY OF NATIONS

This splendid appeal was met by terrible measures of repression. The Japanese authorities showed no mercy, and, to the infinite disappointment of the Koreans, the Western nations took scarcely any notice of what was happening, partly because the facts were not generally known, partly because Europe was engrossed with the making of a so-called Peace Treaty at Versailles, and partly because no government wished to criticize Japan's treatment of her dependency, some fearing no doubt that such criticism might prove to be a boomerang.

Japanese statesmen have very skilfully covered over the facts; they have stated that the reforms introduced in August 1919 were really in contemplation when the independence movement broke out in March and were thereby delayed.[1] But the facts cannot ultimately be concealed, and Japan's handling of Korea in this and a number of other matters simply cannot be explained away.

It is perfectly true that the Japanese occupation has meant great material prosperity. In ten years the area under cultivation increased by 75 per cent., the mineral production by 300 per cent., the railway mileage by 100 per cent., the Government schools by almost 100 per cent. During the ten years from 1910–1920 over 160 million trees have been planted in the great re-afforestation schemes. Law and order have been maintained, brigandage has been put down, sanitation has been improved. But the one thing Korea asks for, the present Japanese Government has no intention whatever of giving. The new Governor-General, Baron Saito, with whom I discussed the whole question when in Korea, is a man of liberal education and really

[1] Even if these reforms were contemplated before the outbreak they are in no sense an adequate answer to the Korean demand for independence.

interested in the good of the people. The policy of Japanization is being pursued in a kindly way. Torture has nearly, if not entirely, come to an end. There is an appearance of peace and plenty. I believe Baron Saito is quite honest in his belief that the Koreans cannot govern themselves, and is trying to govern them in their own interests and not simply in those of Japan. So much the independence movement has taught the governing mind of Japan. What would happen if again the people expressed their demand I dare not predict. But I failed to find among prominent Japanese in government positions any idea whatever that the duty of Japan might be to fit Korea for independence. Few seemed to see that autonomy within the Empire was even possible. The prevailing idea was that Koreans might in some distant future send representatives to sit in the Diet in Tokyo. I could not fail to draw comparisons between the British in Ireland and the Japanese in Korea.[1]

So far as China is concerned the effect of the object lesson may be summed up as follows :—

1. China has seen what Japanese official promises are worth and how little she minds breaking them. Repeatedly did she covenant to observe Korean independence. It is questionable whether she ever meant to observe it.

2. China has also seen how little Western Powers are concerned to see that justice is done to a subject

[1] Personally I cannot see how independence could at once be given to the country without very grave loss. I believe a temporary Japanese occupation, in a different spirit, and with a declared and steadily pursued objective of independence within, say, ten, fifteen or twenty years, might be the best thing for Korea. I very much doubt if Korea could now produce statesmen able to handle the very complex problems of her relation to other nations, and I think independence would only mean virtual dependence on some other Power. At the same time I do not see any immediate prospect of the kind of Japanese tutelage I desiderate.

race, even when a great and practically unanimous national appeal is made to them.

3. China has seen what she takes to be a revelation of the real Japan, the military, domineering Power which stands over her, threatening her very existence. Japan will have to do things very differently before the object lesson of Korea is forgotten in the Far East.

Shantung and the Twenty-One Demands.

It is commonly supposed that the Anglo-Japanese Alliance automatically brought Japan into the Great War. Japanese statesmen have themselves put forward this view. A closer reading of the alliance and a study of the actual facts do not support it. Viscount Ishii stated in America that the Anglo-Japanese Alliance did not, as a matter of fact, involve Japan in the European War. Her object in coming in can be easily read in the light of events. It was a unique opportunity for tightening her hold on China. She was determined not to let German rights in Shantung pass into any other hands than hers. By becoming a belligerent she could easily oust Germany, and gain a foothold in the third of the three great peninsulas that command the entrance to the Chinese capital. Europe was very busy with her own affairs. While she fought, Japan could lay her hand upon China. This she did with steady persistence. Germany's rights in Shantung she claimed as the just reward of her conquest, saving her face by a promise of ultimate return to China. This gave her control of the railway where she at once replaced Chinese officials by Japanese, and placed many more guards on the line than Germany had done. In fact it was quite obvious to all who knew the facts that

JAPAN IN CHINA

Japan meant to stay in Shantung. The policy in Korea which I have described gave additional support to this view.

Not, however, until the presentation of the infamous twenty-one demands was the hand of Japan fully disclosed. This act is now seen by many Japanese statesmen to have been a terrible mistake. I have myself talked with one member of the Cabinet which presented these demands and heard him say that he regarded his action in this matter as the greatest mistake in his life. In fact he has publicly recanted his participation in this act. These demands were divided into five groups. Their original form was greatly altered and they were at first kept secret. In their original form they may be described as follows:—

Group I deals with Japan's demand to take over all the German rights in Shantung, insists on the opening up of fresh centres for foreign trade in the province and concedes to Japan the right of further railway construction.

Group II deals with Manchuria and Eastern Inner Mongolia and is designed to increase the hold of Japan in these regions. Further mining concessions are foreshadowed and the Japanese Government insists on being consulted in regard to loans and concessions and appointment of advisers involving any third Power. That is to say Japan claims absolute priority, not to say a monopoly, for her enterprises in this part of China.

Group III claims Japanese partnership, which would really be predominance, in the famous Hanyehping Iron Company and the mines upon which it depends and other others in the neighbourhood. This concern is the most prosperous one of the kind in China and commands some of the richest supplies.

Group IV is a single article in which the Chinese Government agrees not to cede or lease to any third Power any harbour, bay or island on the Chinese coast. (To appreciate the full significance of this apparently innocuous demand, imagine France trying to force upon England a treaty by which the latter would agree not to cede any Channel port to a third party!)

Group V demands the employment of Japanese as advisers in political, military and financial matters, Japanese participation in the Chinese Police Service, the purchase of a large proportion of her ammunition from Japan, and certain other financial, mining and railway concessions.

The presentation of these demands was carefully timed when Europe was pre-occupied with the war. It was proceeded with in a most high-handed way. An incorrect and modified version was all that was allowed to go to the public. Finally, acceptance was demanded at forty-eight hours' notice backed by a threat of war. Before this ultimatum was launched a few modifications had been agreed to. China had no military strength with which to resist. She could not get any other country to give her any material assistance. She was compelled to embody in treaties all the points on which Japan insisted, save the last group, which China never accepted and Japan never withdrew until the Washington Conference nearly seven years later.

By this means Japan, following the example set her by European nations, gained "legal sanction" for her aggression in Shantung, extended her hold over China's resources and territory in other directions and virtually stepped into the position of paramount Power in Chinese affairs. Had the fifth group been accepted China would, to an even greater extent, have given up her independence.

JAPAN IN CHINA 111

It is a matter for great satisfaction that it has now been finally withdrawn; for it was hanging, as Putnam Weale put it, like a Sword of Damocles over China's head.

In the final form, then, in which the treaties were signed, Japan's demands seem much less objectionable than they were at first. It has even been urged that the more extreme statement (and in particular the demands of Group V) was made in order that Japan might have something to bargain with. This may be true, but if so it was a serious tactical mistake. Japan, by this action, roused the spirit of the whole nation in bitter antagonism, greatly aggravated when the ultimatum was presented. Later modifications did not remove this first impression, and China will not for many a long day forget what she felt as so bitter a humiliation and affront. Japan's true policy would have been to win the confidence and friendship of China. These she sacrificed and these it will be very hard to regain.

China's Entry into the Great War.

Passing over certain other negotiations, let us look at the way in which the peculiar ambitions of Japan in regard to China affected China's policy when she was asked to join America in breaking off diplomatic relations with Germany and finally in declaring war. There again China was the catspaw in a game in which she was bound to suffer.

Quite early in the war China made a proposal to enter as one of the Allied nations. This was her last resort, after trying other methods by which she might be a partner in driving Germany out of Shantung, so avoiding the alienation of the German rights in that province to Japan. This proposal was not entertained, Japan, as we have seen, having "other fish to fry." It appears to have been turned down by Great Britain, but what reasons were given I cannot say. It was China's last effort to become an active agent in the disposition of her own affairs in Shantung. Mr. Millard gives particulars of this and two other attempts by China to come into the war prior to the end of 1915. On the last occasion Japan revealed her hand, and urged that developments in China were a paramount interest to her, and "*she must keep a firm hand*. Japan could not regard with equanimity the organization of an efficient Chinese army such as would be required for her active participation in the war, nor could Japan fail to regard with uneasiness a liberation of the economic activities of a nation of 400,000,000 people." [1]

To those who studied the Far Eastern situation it became increasingly clear that a victory for the Allies would mean that Japan would gain a firmer hold in China. It was in order to avoid this, and not in order to oppose German aggression and to protest against her methods of warfare, that China finally came into the war. It may, however, be questioned whether even in this matter she was well advised. When America severed her relations with Germany she advised other neutrals, and China among them, to follow her example. Japan was opposed to China's taking such action, partly because she did not wish to have China represented at the Peace Conference. In one of the documents published by the Soviet Government this matter is very clearly stated, and there Viscount Motono, on behalf of Japan, expressed his willingness to urge China to come into the war

[1] *Saturday Evening Post*, April 28, 1917.

only if the Allied Powers would support Japan in respect of Shantung and the Pacific Islands. The other Allies, however, and individual citizens of Allied countries who had weight with the Chinese Government, continued to urge China forward. Mr. Blythe, an American who was in Peking at the time, has thus described the campaign :—

"For hours and hours, day and night, Peking resounded with speeches to timid Chinese made by these urgent Americans and the two invaluable Australians (Dr. Morrison and W. H. Donald), urging, forcing, begging, cajoling and shoving the Chinese who were needful to toe the mark. There was no rest. There was no soft-pedal business. It was a big, hard, two-fisted campaign, and he who dallied was a dastard and he who doubted was roundly damned." [1]

Many Chinese, especially the young foreign-educated men, doubtless believed that China, in following America's lead, was taking a step for international right. The note sent to Germany (February 9, 1917) explicitly based China's action on this ground. But the real influences at work were the pressure of foreign nations, in particular America, whom the Chinese regarded as pacific and as a friend of their own, and the desire to have a seat at the Peace Conference in order that China's claims in Shantung might be recognized. China had not any real interest in the war issues as they were seen by us in the West.

We have already seen how the actual declaration of war by China became the source of a very serious crisis in China's internal affairs, and led to the division of North from South, which has not yet been fully healed. Looked at from China's point of view I cannot feel that she had anything

[1] *Saturday Evening Post*, April 28, 1917.

to gain. Japan was again opposed to the action in the first place, not from consideration for China, but for reasons similar to those already given. Japan had, however, succeeded in extracting promises from her allies of their support of her claims in China and on the strength of these she was more ready to advise China to proceed. China was assured by her new allies that they would stand by her in true friendship, but all the time they had entered into secret pacts to support Japan in despoiling her—all, that is, save America, who, as events showed, was unable at the Peace Conference to make good her protestation of goodwill.

In Mr. Millard's review of the situation, in spite of his strong sympathies with America in bringing China into the war, I find an opinion of a Chinese of high standing which has been wonderfully borne out by the event. He said to Mr. Millard, among other things :—

"I think I have observed among the other nations a disposition to consider their own positions and interests, and so we Chinese may be excused for thinking first about this war in terms of the interests and security of China. You say we can trust the United States, especially President Wilson, to get justice for China at the Peace Conference. As to that, your Government has always talked very well about China, but at the pinch it usually has left her in the lurch by refusing to take any active part in aiding her, or even to enforce your own policies here. As to President Wilson, he is but a man and will die in time, and his time of office ends in a short while. . . . We do not now trust Great Britain or France, because of their apparent acceptance of Japan's policy towards China. We cannot afford to repose trust in the United States until it proves to us that it has the will and the power to

JAPAN IN CHINA 115

help us. . . . Separated from Great Britain and France we do not believe that America will be strong enough to put a check on Japan." [1]

Thus while many of the best minds in China were opposed to the policy, while it was certain to strike a terrible blow at China's unity and at the development of democratic government and give new power to her own internal enemies, the military chieftains, China was hurried into the war by her so-called friends. Well might she pray to be saved from her friends. Germany could have struck her no blow which compares with that dealt her by the Allies.

JAPAN'S "SPECIAL POSITION" IN CHINA.

Japan followed up the successes gained with the European Allies by sending a special envoy to America. It was very important for her to secure from the United States some recognition of her paramount interests in China, in order, if possible, to prevent American interference with her schemes when the Far Eastern question came under discussion at the Peace Conference. The plans for securing this are revealed in another of the documents issued by that indiscreet Government in Moscow! A despatch from the Russian Ambassador at Tokyo, October 22, 1917 states that in the negotiations by Viscount Ishii (the envoy referred to above) "the question at issue is not some special concession to Japan in these or other parts of China, but Japan's special position in China as a whole." In the light of this revelation we read the famous Lansing-Ishii Agreement—(November 2, 1917). This document was to have been published simultaneously in Tokyo and Washington. By breaking

[1] Op. cit., p. 128.

the terms of this arrangement Japan put it out in such a way as to make it appear as a diplomatic triumph for herself. The carefully-worded clause in which Mr. Lansing believed he had uttered no more than a platitude was, by a slight mis-translation into Chinese, made to appear like a concession of all that Japan asked for. The clause read as follows:—

"The Governments of the United States and Japan recognize that territorial propinquity creates special relations between countries, and, consequently, the Government of the United States recognizes that Japan has special interests in China, particularly in that part to which her possessions are contiguous."

The publication of this document created a sensation in Peking and throughout China. Here, it seemed, was America, her one friend, stepping aside and giving Japan a free hand in the exploitation of the country. Her worst fears seemed to be justified.

Mr. Lansing did his best to correct what seemed to be clearly a misapprehension caused by the methods I have described. But it cannot be said that he was wholly successful. The Chinese are too accustomed to the method of denying in public what you affirm in private. The shock had been administered, and Japan seemed to have gained all she wanted. An agreement touching her at a most vital spot had been concluded between two of her allies without even consulting her—and one of those allies was her last hope in regard to the redress of her grievances at the Peace Conference.

We shall see in the next chapter how Japan followed up this advantage, and how Versailles confirmed the worst fears of China in regard to the worthlessness of professions of friendship, even from her best friend. What we have already seen has served to show to what an extent China has been used by the Powers in the last few years, and how step by step Japan has secured a position which the Chinese feel to be threatening their very existence as a nation. Is it any wonder that anti-Japanese boycotts have spread to every part of China ?

CHAPTER VII

JAPAN IN CHINA (*continued*)

FINANCIAL PENETRATION

THE methods of economic imperialism which have been perfected by the more industrialized nations of the West have been taken over in recent years by Japan and applied very thoroughly in her dealings with China. In this action Japan has aroused the enmity not only of Chinese but also of other foreigners in China. This, as we shall see, is due partly to the fact that Japan has become a very active and efficient commercial competitor, and partly to the fact that she has not kept to the agreements she has made in regard to China. Japan seems to Western merchants not to be "playing the game," even this common game of grab, for which there are certain rules, more or less observed, among the great commercial nations of the West.

It will be convenient to give a rough classification of the methods of economic imperialism as seen in China, the order corresponding in a general way to the actual developments in history.

1. The first stage is to bring one's wares and to try to open up trade. If, as in the case of China, the country does not wish to buy one's goods, she must be made to see, by force if necessary, that she cannot afford to refuse them. The process is especially blameworthy where the goods are actually harmful as they were in the case of opium, but

I cannot myself regard it as defensible even where the goods are useful.

2. The uncertainties of such trade when it depends upon the occasional visits of ships from abroad and the advantages that come to the merchant from living in the country with which he trades, or sending his agent there, create a demand for "rights of residence." This leads to the opening of "treaty ports" where foreigners may trade and live, and to the leasing of property, known as a "concession" or "foreign settlement," where the foreigners can make their own arrangements and live in their own way.

3. The fact that the laws of China are very different from those of Western lands, are ill-administered in many cases and involve punishments which we regard as cruel and unjustifiable, leads to the further demand for extra-territoriality —that is to say the "right" to administer the law of the foreign State in the settlements and the exclusion of all subjects of foreign nations from Chinese law. This brings them under consular jurisdiction and involves an *imperium in imperio*.

4. In view of the perplexing state of the internal and external customs of China, a further demand arises (1842) for a fixed tariff, and this, being fixed by the foreign nations, is arranged in the interests of increasing their trade rather than in the interests of the revenue of China. If we assume the right to trade and the right for fair conditions of trade, this tariff interference may seem to be inevitable, but we have only to consider how England would feel if France tried to insist on certain tariff limitations, to realize how Chinese feel on this question.

5. In order to see that these tariff regulations are put into force in a country where the

central government is weak, the oversight of the customs is put under foreigners and thus, beginning with the time of the Taiping rebellion, we see a vast system built up throughout China, managed by foreigners (under treaty regulations) and yielding a large revenue to China. This revenue subsequently becomes the security for interest on foreign loans.[1]

6. A further stage is reached when China begins to think of opening up her natural resources, building railways, factories and harbours. The suggestion for such enterprises has again come from the foreigner, and he must be called in to supply the brains, the materials and the capital. Treaties provide for such concessions and the companies concerned claim and obtain certain "rights" in order that they may have security for their investment of capital. Moreover these treaties in certain cases include clauses specifically stating that the material must be bought in the country whose citizens receive the concession or make the loan. Thus a monopoly in the interest of one nation is created in one place, and for another in another place.

7. These " rights " having been secured by treaty and thus given a certain legal validity, whatever we may think about the moral sanction, it is quite obvious that they must be insisted upon even if in doing so individual Chinese suffer. Not to do so would be to set international law at nought! If debts are not repaid they must be collected and military measures are thus justified. It is fairly certain that in a country that has resisted all these

[1] It is only right to add that the customs service has been administered by high-minded men, who have genuinely worked for China's good. It has a fine record, and if all foreign interference in China were of this order there is no doubt China would be thankful for the help given, rather than resentful and afraid of it.

advances and does not really believe that this foreign trade is an advantage to her, there will be cases of vigorous resistance and even repudiation of the " rights " obtained as stated.

8. It is not, however, only for economic development that loans are required. The government itself needs money in order to protect China against this continuous encroachment. Where can she get it but from the countries that are menacing her ? So large-scale loans for public purposes have to be raised. The income from the customs, the salt, and the post office must be mortgaged to pay interest and redemption on such loans. So the shackles become heavier in the very effort to shake them off. Big business, big banking houses, and big governments with big forces behind them stand ready to assist China according to the programme of the vicious circle, and on the principle of each for himself and the devil take the hindmost. It is not necessary to suggest who is the hindmost in this instance.

9. It is a very easy stage from this to the policy of "spheres of influence" which, as we have seen, was followed for a few terrible years by the Western Powers in their dealings with China. It was little less than an agreement among thieves, and they seemed only to be waiting their chance to swallow up each his allotted morsel.

10. It was at this point that the situation was relieved by the statement and acceptance, with more or less reluctance, of Mr. Hay's policy of the open door. Some Powers did, I believe, wish to see this policy definitely adopted and honestly maintained. Japan and Russia do not seem to have been among those. For Japan there was every excuse. She had seen the Western Powers rushing in on their prey. What reason had she to

think that they really meant to deal differently by China ? Was not this simply a new phase in Western hypocrisy ? At any rate so far as the Power nearest to her was concerned there was very considerable ground for such a surmise. It is true that for a short period prior to the war with Russia, Japan did espouse the policy of the open door, only to deny it (in practice though not in theory) as soon as she had replaced Russia in Manchuria.

11. The policy of the open door led to that of the consortium. No longer was each nation to be rushing in to gain separate advantage, by making loans, which on account of the supposed poor security are always at rates very advantageous to the lenders. Obviously this cut-throat policy would not in the end work to the advantage of foreign investors. How far the desire to see it modified in China's favour really influenced things I am unable to say. It was a case where self-interest and the interest of the client did seem in some respects to be identical. However, the terms offered to China were not much better, although investors virtually had for security (1) the assurance that the combined efforts of all the great capitalist States would be used to see that China paid up, (2) the immense wealth and resourcefulness of the Chinese people themselves, and (3) agreements whereby a first charge on China's richest revenues was to be the meeting of these foreign obligations ! Nevertheless, loans are concluded on terms that give frequently a return of 7, 8, 9 or even 10 per cent. and not infrequently at a price of considerably less than 100 per cent., and in such a way that large flotation expenses are allowed, for the government or borrowing party receives say only 90 or 95 per cent. of the total sum subscribed or of the nominal capital.

JAPAN IN CHINA 123

12. The agreement for loans only by a consortium of the banks in the main lending countries has always been difficult to arrive at and enforce. China has felt that she was only being exploited on a larger scale and that she could no longer play off one country against another. She has very naturally feared a complete financial dictatorship. There has often been some party ready to offer what China felt to be better terms, as in the famous Crisp loan (1912), concluded in face of the agreement for the common action by all the Powers. Japan in recent years has gained an undesirable reputation as being more ready to break through any such understanding than was any other Power. Mr. Millard gives a list of no fewer than 55 loans made by Japan to China between 1909 and 1918.[1] A good many were short term ones and have been repaid frequently by contracting another "reorganization loan," discount and expenses being collected again and again when such loans had to be repaid and reorganized.

13. The final stage in this progression seems to be a large measure of economic dictatorship. The policy of the country comes under the influence of the Power or Powers who have the largest financial interests. One may say that no country now thinks in terms of annexing China or parts of China, unless it be Japan with regard to Manchuria and Eastern Inner Mongolia. But annexation is too costly a process if the same result can be obtained in other ways. The aim of economic imperialism is financial profit to be made out of the country. It is quite possible to maintain that China will in the end be better off through economic interchange with other countries, and that much of our merchandise goes to raising the standard of living and increasing the

[1] Op. cit., pp. 187-92

happiness of Chinese. But we should indeed be self-deceived if we allowed ourselves to suppose that China's interests have been the dominating motive in this long process. I have seen displayed on the walls of a Chinese city the advertisement of Dr. Williams' Pink Pills for Pale People. Now it is quite possible that pale Chinese may benefit by taking the pink pills. But I cannot stretch my imagination so far as to think of Dr. Williams as a kindly philanthropist eager to bring back the colour into the faces of pale Celestials. He, whoever he may be, is in China in order to secure some of the few coins possessed by these same pallid persons to distribute among the shareholders in his company. Nor can I think that the British-American Tobacco Company adopts the slogan "a cigarette in the mouth of every Chinese" because it has any deep conviction that the Chinese will be the better men physically or morally for using British-American tobacco. No, we must admit the motive is gain, and it is still true that an evil tree cannot bring forth good fruit. Although there are many honest foreigners doing business in China, and although not a few of these really do want to serve China and have come to respect her people and to feel with them in their difficulties and distresses, the financial penetration of China is, taken as a whole, a poor way of bringing China into the family of nations.

This record raises in an acute form the question as to what are the sovereign rights of a free people. How far is a nation morally bound by treaties which secure by force the so-called rights of other nations,—rights which the people of the nation concerned regard rather as wrongs? But these issues carry us too far afield for our present purpose.

Now Japan, as I have said, has seen how Western

JAPAN IN CHINA

nations got into China. In her own "spheres of influence" and outside them she has steadily and skilfully pursued the same policy. She has not infrequently beaten the West at her own game. In certain respects she has used methods which Westerners do not like to admit that their Governments ever use. For example, in Manchuria there has been a system of espionage, accompanied by many tricks which are plainly underhand, for keeping out foreign trade. Here is one instance out of many. An American travelling for his firm commits his case of samples to the Japanese-managed South Manchurian Railway [1] only to have it returned after much delay without a single sample in it. There are too many instances of such happenings for them to be written down as mere coincidences, or due to the work of isolated criminals.

Japan, too, is always on the spot. Her nationals move in and out in China in a way that Europeans and Americans cannot. She watches the situation far more closely, and this was, of course, specially true of the war period. For these reasons China fears Japanese aggression even more than she fears that of Europe or America. The growing hold of Japan, through finance, on the political situation in China, is felt as a very real menace to China's development. This is peculiarly felt by the younger and more democratic element, because they see that Japan is concerned to prevent her neighbour from becoming a successful republic. They argue, not without reason, that, as Japan has built her financial and political success upon a very pronounced type of autocracy with emperor-worship at the centre, she will not be pleased to see the

[1] This railway company is really a general exploiting company with mines and trading rights, and is controlled by the Japanese Government.

sister country show a better type of civilization under democratic institutions. Such an example would naturally give impetus to the revolutionary elements in Japan. Now Japanese statesmen can point to China and say: "See what a failure democracy is in an Oriental country like ours. Clearly it is not suited to our conditions."

There is therefore a strong case for those who would use Japan's economic advantage to keep China relatively weak, and it is not always easy to persuade even enlightened Japanese that their country's true policy is rather to strengthen China and help it to become stable both financially and politically.

Japan's *apologia* is well stated by Viscount Motono in an interview in September 1917, when he said that Japan had adopted the policy of economic imperialism in self-defence and as a precautionary measure, and would be prepared to abandon it if the other principal nations would do the same.[1] All I can say is that Japan has not had any adequate proof that this condition has been met, and that therefore it is unfair to single her out for special blame.

At the same time it is true that Japan has staked out enormous claims in China, that she has used her power in a way that virtually closed the door which was professedly open, and that Chinese feel that she is, at the moment, their most dangerous neighbour. This is not to say that Chinese have any convictions that the motives or policies of other nations are better than those of Japan. The exception is in the case of America, which, as we shall see later, has won the regard and confidence of China in a rather special way.

[1] Millard, op. cit., p. 259.

JAPAN IN CHINA

THE DEMORALIZATION OF CHINA.

It is now unfortunately necessary to refer to another matter in which Japan has gained an unenviable reputation. Britain's record first in forcing China to receive opium and then in bringing this evil traffic to an end has already been mentioned. Those who look upon China mainly as a market are very critical of this second act which they maintain was a piece of foolish idealism pressed by a few misguided faddists. This side of the picture can be looked at in Bland's *Recent Events and Present Policies in China* (chapter xv). Biassed as this presentation is, and containing some serious misstatements, I think it should be read by any student of the question as saying the best that can be said for a thoroughly bad case. Even supposing Mr. Bland's argument that opium never can be eradicated from China to be true, it remains a matter of deep thankfulness that Britain is no longer a gainer by that which brings misery and degradation to many millions in China. It cannot, however, be forgotten that for many years merchants of British nationality, though many not of British race, were making huge profits from this demoralizing trade. It was not simply an instance of trade for private profit but of trade that actually did harm to the country concerned. The fullest statement of the matter is to be found in Mr. Joshua Rowntree's *The Imperial Drug Trade*, written before the trade was ended.[1]

Since the formal closing of the Indo-Chinese opium traffic Japan has stepped into the shoes of Great Britain, and vast quantities of the drug (largely in the far more dangerous form of morphia)

[1] See also several interesting allusions in J. A. Hobson's *Life of Cobden*.

have reached China in recent years, through the Japanese post office, and through Japanese pedlars and minor traders. Very careful reports have been gathered from all parts of China as to the prevalence of the morphia habit, and no one can fail to be convinced of Japanese complicity in this matter, when it is seen how the chief areas of the use of the drug correspond with those where Japanese influence is strongest. I should not, myself, assume that the Japanese Government deliberately fostered this trade, which is mainly illicit. Nevertheless, as a certain direct revenue comes to the State, a definite blame is thereby fixed upon it, and I do not think the Government can be acquitted of culpable negligence. The Chinese draw the not unnatural conclusion that Japan is trying to keep China weak by deliberately pandering to her well-known weakness in this matter.[1]

This conclusion seems to be supported by another very disquieting fact, I mean the introduction of many Japanese prostitutes into those parts of China where Japan is paramount. Here again, and even more emphatically, I would acquit the Government of a deliberate design for undermining the manhood of China. But young Chinese feel this matter most keenly, and if Japan is to win back the confidence and friendship of China it is high time she dealt vigorously with this traffic in vice. I am not, of course, saying that China is free from the "social evil." A reading, for example, of the recent admirable *Social Survey of Peking* shows in what way it thrives in a purely Chinese city as part of

[1] One must sincerely hope that the recent action of the League of Nations will mean a large reduction in the export of opium and its derivatives from Japan to China. At least it gives Japan a chance to show whether she really cares for China's good in this matter or not. It is, of course, too soon to say how she will interpret and enforce this action. Cf. Millard, pp. 207-17.

the national life and quite independent of any foreign influence. But there are ways in which Japan has practised the evil which have been unknown in China, and there can be no doubt that the introduction of Japanese customs into China has put fresh temptation in the way of Chinese young men.

Another charge made against Japan is that she has used the Chinese bandits as a means of keeping up internal disorder, and that these persons are constantly supplied with Japanese arms and munitions. This is certainly commonly believed among Chinese. Personally I have no evidence which proves the official complicity of Japan in this unlawful traffic, though it seems quite clear that individual Japanese traders are prepared to make profits out of the sale of arms which they know will be used to continue the state of unrest in the country. I should not be prepared to credit the accounts of Japanese soldiers in disguise co-operating with Chinese bandits, as meaning anything more than that there are bad characters in the Japanese armies as in all others, and that they are ready to gain through the unsettled state of a country where there is much irregular fighting. Similar instances could be found, for example, in Ireland and need not be taken as meaning government complicity in such actions.

One further point that may be mentioned is the undoubted fact that Chinese carrying on unlawful trade in drugs and other things frequently seek and obtain Japanese protection, especially in the province of Fukien. Japan is not alone in this matter, but I think there is no doubt that she is the chief sinner, partly, no doubt, because many Chinese (e.g. in Formosa) are Japanese subjects.

A more serious charge is that Japan has been

130 CHINA IN THE FAMILY OF NATIONS

ready to make loans to Chinese militarists or sectional governments with the object of keeping up internal strife, so preventing China from forming a strong united government. Discussing this question with well-informed Japanese the charge was virtually admitted, while I was assured that Japan's policy in this matter had now changed, and that she intended only to allow her subjects to lend, or herself to lend money to a government that represented, as far as could be ascertained, the whole of the country. If Japan has come to see that it is to her own interest to have a strong, friendly and united China rather than a weak, embittered and disunited one, we shall certainly see a very marked change in Japan's policy in the next few years. Before giving my reasons for hoping that such a change is actually taking place let me bring the story of Japan's relations with China up-to-date and summarize the position as I found it during my recent visit, so that the extent of China's distrust of her powerful neighbour may be vividly realized.

EVENTS SINCE THE CLOSE OF THE EUROPEAN WAR.

China, as we have seen, purchased at a great cost her right to a seat at the Peace Conference in Versailles. Was the gain worth the price? All the world knows what happened in those epoch-making days as the dictators of the world drew new maps, fixed economic conditions, determined the fates of peoples, as if they were playing a game of chess. China was one of the victims of the policy of opportunism and revenge and self-gratification that laid the foundations of the post-war world on shifting sand. Japan played her cards with consummate skill. She was determined to

maintain her hold in Shantung and to get the
imprimatur of the Allies for her predatory acts.
One can scarcely fail to be amused by the theory
advanced by Japan in regard to Port Arthur,
Manchuria and Shantung that the death of Japanese
soldiers on the soil of a foreign Power with whom
she was not at war should give a certain right to
her to hold that territory as her own. It is as if
England had claimed that the blood of her soldiers
who died at Waterloo gave her a presumptive right
to take Belgium into the British Empire! However
little argument could be found to support the position, Japan gained her point. President Wilson
had just stood firm over Fiume and driven Italy
out of the inner circle. I suppose he felt that by
a similar and no less obviously just stand over
Shantung he would drive out Japan, and this he
could not afford to do. Everything must go in
order that the League of Nations might be set up.

Whatever the reasons, the result was utterly
disastrous. I was in Paris shortly after the fateful
decision had been made and heard the story of
its reception by the Chinese delegation, from several
who were present. The news was brought while a
dinner was in progress. It came from a Press
representative. So absolutely did the Chinese rely
on the friendship of America and her power to see
justice done that the first message was not credited,
and Mr. Lansing was called up and asked if he
could confirm or deny it. Although it had reached
the Press, Mr. Lansing knew nothing about it.
Nevertheless the incredible was true. Japan's
" rights " in Shantung were to be ratified by the
world. One Chinese flung himself on the floor in
a paroxysm of despair and rage. One of my informants told me how he looked across the table at
a military attaché trained in a Western military

academy. He saw an expression come into his face that could not be mistaken. He was registering a secret vow to devote every ounce of his strength to the sacred task of building up in China a military power so strong that China would have to be listened to in the councils of the nations. The appeal to justice had failed before the court of humanity. China's millions must now try the only other way and speak in the one language the modern world could understand.

Throughout China there was utter dismay. The news seemed not simply like the death-knell to China and the beginning of a period of unlimited Japanese exploitation. It spelled for China the utter hollowness of the professions of the Allies in their high-sounding war aims. This "Christian" West stood before the eyes of "Heathen" China condemned, by her own voice, of hypocrisy and callous indifference to the plain justice of a weak and long-suffering nation's case. China had trusted to the goodwill at least of America and of the better mind of England. Her trust was misplaced. Could she ever trust again?

People who speak enthusiastically of the triumph of the Washington Conference do not remember the background on which it had to work. Think of the long history of Western and Japanese aggression culminating in the great betrayal of Versailles, and the hard-won gains at Washington seem but a minute compensation for this long tale of wrong. Is it to be expected that all at once China will accept this one small step as the sign of a complete repentance on the part either of Japan or of the West? Against great opposition and with a pathetic further appeal to the sense of justice of the great Powers, China urged the reconsideration of her claims at Washington. At last it was agreed that

JAPAN IN CHINA

they might be discussed outside the actual meeting. Japan finally accepted a considerable part of the Chinese claim, and agreed, for a consideration, to hand back to China the German "rights" in Shantung and to withdraw the unratified demands of Group V. But these gains seemed to China to be wrung out of a reluctant Japan who yielded them only because the conscience of the West was at last aroused, and when very strong pressure was brought to bear upon her. I was told in Japan that there had been an intention by the government from the beginning to yield this much, and that she did not at once state her willingness because she feared that there would be a spirit of bargaining and that she would have to give more than her first offer. This may be true, but even so, I believe she would have been well advised to come forward with a generous offer, and so do something to create a new psychological situation. As it is, the feeling towards Japan has been but little bettered by Japan's yielding, partly for the reasons stated and partly because at the same time Japan showed herself more unyielding on the question of tariff-revision than any of the other Powers. In this matter China put forward claims that were not at all unreasonable, and that would have met with a much more reasonable response from the other Powers, had not Japan insisted on giving China only a very small amount of what she asked.

It must, therefore, be said that the feelings in China towards Japan were not materially improved by the Washington Conference, at any rate up to last summer, and there still remains the problem much as I have stated it in these pages, a problem which must be solved if China is to find the place she seeks and to which she is entitled in the family of nations.

134 CHINA IN THE FAMILY OF NATIONS

Present Position Summed Up.

In 1905, when I first went to China, Japan was fighting China's battle against Russia and her recent policy towards China had been most friendly. She had strongly upheld the policy of the open door and of Chinese integrity. In negotiating the Anglo-Japanese Alliance, Count Hayashi had said: "We entirely agree with the British policy in Eastern countries. That is to say we wish to maintain the territorial integrity of China and the principle of equal opportunity."[1] The result of this policy, continued with Japan's success in war and in peaceful adaptation to new conditions, led China to turn eagerly and even enthusiastically to Japan for help. Japanese instructors were asked over in hundreds to the new colleges, military academies and technical schools in China; Japanese text-books were imported wholesale; Japanese colleges and universities were crowded with Chinese students; Japanese ideas were current through the length and breadth of the land.

The change came very soon. Students came back from Tokyo speaking of many indignities which they had suffered. Japan showed her hand in Korea, and in other acts. The feeling against Japan became marked even before the Great War. Perhaps the revolution was a chief factor in the change, for the new democratic ideas were clearly not congenial to the Japanese authorities and Japan came then under a more direct criticism from some of those who were leading Young China.

To-day we see Japan held up not as the example to be followed, but as the example to be avoided, no longer a light to guide, but a beacon to warn.

---

[1] Quoted in *The Foreign Relations of China*, p. 184.

JAPAN IN CHINA

This, as we have seen, is due to the following causes :—

1. Japan's activities in Korea and Formosa.
2. Japan's hold on Manchuria.
3. Japan's seizure of German rights in Shantung.
4. Japan's demands on, and economic hold in, the Yangtse Valley.
5. Japan's strong influence in Fukien.
6. The belief that Japan is deliberately seeking to undermine the manhood of the nation.
7. The belief that Japan is determined to secure a prior place in China, to dictate her policy to her and virtually to treat her as a subject people.
8. The belief that Japan intends to drain away, for her own advantage, as much as she can of the mineral and other wealth of China.
9. Behind all these causes lies a deep and almost universal distrust of Japan's sincerity when she professes friendliness, coupled with a sense that Japan, who should have acted as a brother to her nearest of kin, has betrayed China and used her advantage to exploit and dominate her.

Wherever an explanation of any of the above points favourable to Japan is urged in China to-day one is met by this distrust which refuses to accept any but the worst interpretation of the facts, a very serious and intractable symptom.

Japan's case can be stated somewhat as follows :—

1. She has a rapidly increasing population which she cannot (apparently) accommodate on her own territory. Australia, Canada and the United States agree in excluding Japanese. Where is she to look for

expansion if not to adjacent parts of the Asiatic continent ? How can her nationals go there and put themselves under a government that gives them insufficient protection and no adequate security in their economic enterprises ?

In regard to this point it is argued with a good deal of truth that, with better methods of cultivation and so forth, Japan could deal with her growing population for at least another fifty years, and also that, as a matter of simple fact, Japanese cannot successfully compete on equal terms with Chinese and are not colonizing Formosa, Korea, Manchuria, etc., in any way that really solves her population question. The Japanese Government has to create specially favourable conditions for her colonists, and in the main they are the capitalists, exploiters, directors and police in these areas rather than ordinary colonists. That is to say, Japan is in China and Korea as the British in India rather than as the British in Australia or the Chinese in the Straits Settlements.

2. Japan, in order to develop her industries, must have an assured supply of raw materials larger than she can get from her own country. She cannot have this without a direct financial interest in industrial concerns in the country of supply, because other buyers would possibly overbid her and take away what is really her life-blood. Moreover, the holding of large financial stakes in China, with her present unstable government, is impossible unless some political guarantee is given, as all other creditor countries agree. This leads to military pressure, the stationing of garrisons in areas where financial interests are large and the demand for special privileges.

3. Granted that, ideally, it ought to be possible to secure the raw material needed without using

these accessory methods, Japan is faced by the fact that European Powers have used them, and she has no reason to suppose that they mean to desist. Therefore she has an example which goes to prove that she will be cut out in the China markets if she herself does not go one better. It might be urged that China would deal fairly with Japan if the latter forsook the methods of exploitation, but what reason has Japan to think that her competitors would do the same ? Would she not simply be left in the lurch and laughed at for her idealism in a world of predatory nations ?

4. Waiving the question as to whether Japan has or has not kept up the internal dissensions in China, she may well say that her neighbour has not yet shown that she can deal with her own internal problems successfully in the light of the new conditions of the modern world. She is like a man with a very trim garden, weeded and tended with meticulous care, whose neighbour lets his garden run wild. He is sorely tempted to jump over the wall and root up the dandelions before they begin to scatter their seeds all over his well-kept ground. Of course it is quite possible to say that China regards some of those brilliantly coloured flowers which Japan tends with infinite care, emperor-worship, militarism, a narrowly patriotic education, as nothing but the rankest weeds. But from Japan's point of view, China's failure to work out any ordered system of government seems a constant danger right at her doors—a danger which she regards as justification for some interference.

These four broad classes of reasons cannot, in my view, justify Japan's policy, nor do they entirely explain it. There is in Japan a section who are blatantly and aggressively imperialistic, which looks to a Japanese hegemony in Asia and even believes

138 CHINA IN THE FAMILY OF NATIONS

that Japan is one day to rule the world. The Black Dragon Society is the meeting-place and symbol of such extremists. Their avowed aim is to dominate the whole of China, to unite the Orient under the banner of Japan, to challenge Western supremacy in the world and to become the great world Power of the future. The ideas of this society are set forth in Putnam Weale's *Fight for the Republic of China*, and I do not propose to deal with it in full. I regard it as a phase of Japanese life, due to her phenomenal success during the last half century, a case of national swelled-head, similar to that which we saw in a certain section of Germany prior to the Great War, and similar to what is now happening in France. I do not minimize its importance, for, even as in these other instances, it may have the most disastrous influence and consequences for Asia and for the whole world. But I do not wish to assume that Japanese policy has been in the main directed by these extremists. I think these are strong reasons, according to ordinary political reasoning, for such a policy even without calling in this element. I want rather to show that there is yet another section of opinion in Japan, utterly opposed to the idea of the Black Dragon Society. This is challenging the actual policy of the government which may be based much more upon such reasons as the four I have stated. It is to this group in Japan that I look with chief hope.

What is the Real Japan?

I said earlier that there are two Japans. In fact there are at least three. There is the militarist, imperialist Japan; there is the conservative, constitutional Japan, and there is the progressive, pacifist Japan. The first and second are in partial alliance, but by no means in agreement. The third is in an attitude of revolt towards both of the others. One reason for the apparent contradiction of Japanese policy and for the breaches of faith in her foreign relations is to be found in the conflict between the first two Japans. The constitution is not really democratic. The Mikado is supreme in name, though actually under the guidance of the Genro, or Elder Statesmen. These men, of whom now only two survive, have skilfully guided Japan through the dangerous and difficult waters she has had to navigate since she came into the family of nations. It is small wonder that they are respected and trusted and have come to wield an almost autocratic power. The Diet is under the leadership of men who, while respecting the Genro nevertheless are trying to enlarge the area of real popular government. The late Premier Hara was an example of such men. Himself a conservative of the Seiyukai party, he recognized that popular opinion could not be neglected. He stood for the civil as against the military party, but recognized that Japan's power in diplomacy depended upon her military efficiency. An instance of his methods will illuminate the policy of the constitutional party in Japan. When he took office for the last time he demanded a change in the law whereby the heads of the Army and Navy must always be professional soldiers. He let it be known that he was not prepared to take office again unless the right of direct approach to the throne were withdrawn from these officials. That is to say, he was steadily working for a fundamental change which would put the civil power in real control of Japan's foreign policy. His untimely death brought an end to this scheme, but it is to be hoped that the big political parties will continue to press for these reforms. Not infrequently while the civil authority has given a certain undertaking and followed a certain policy the military authority has taken an opposite course and, because of its direct access to the throne and therefore its power over the budget, Japan has been "given away" in public, and the military have won the day as against the civil authorities. Among the younger statesmen in Japan there are not a few who are deeply chagrined at any such action and who greatly distrust the military power. At the same time most of these are unwilling to take a strong line against it partly because they see that Japan must maintain its military forces at maximum strength if she is to make her voice heard in the counsels of the nations, and partly because they feel that any strong action will only lead to disaster as such great power rests in the hands of the militarists.

It is to the third element that I look with greater hope. The leaders of this section are to be found among Members of Parliament who are not connected with either of the great parties, labour leaders and scholars. I have had the opportunity of meeting a number of these, and I found them courageous, far-sighted and broad-minded men who in a number of cases have suffered for their principles and may at any time suffer again. They share the aspirations of the progressive leaders in other parts of the world. They are intensely opposed to Japan's imperialistic acts. Broadly speaking, they are out for a measure of manhood suffrage, a programme of disarmament, a policy in Korea that would lead to ultimate independence (some would go for immediate independence), a friendly policy in all dealings with China and a reversal of anything like exploitation and military occupation, a complete reversal of the educational system so far as it inculcates a purely nationalistic point of view and seeks to instil material and militaristic ideas, an advanced policy of labour legislation looking, if may be, to some degree of democratic control in industry.

I am under no illusion as to the strength of this party. In the country districts and among the less educated people it probably has very few adherents. In the big industrial centres like Osaka and Kobé it is strongly supported. A professor in the Imperial University said that a considerable majority of the students there would vote for giving Korea her independence. There are men and some women of great ability who hold such views as those I have mentioned. But the dice are heavily loaded against them. In the last resort the constitutionalists and the militarists would stand together against them. The Japanese constitution gives no real power to the democracy. How can they make their will effective short of a violent revolution? That method would not appeal to more than a very small minority, and could be instantly crushed by the ruling caste who are vigilant and relentless. The Press is closely watched and censored. News of what is happening in China, for example, only reaches most people in the form in which the government wish them to see it. There is little hope of any immediate success for these reformers. But they have the patience of the East. They are determined to go on. They believe in the power of true ideas. They are touching some of the most vital points in the life of Japan, the Universities, the industrial centres, the new womanhood. I believe their success is not so far away as their opponents think. I do not anticipate a sudden change, but I do anticipate a steady and a considerable one. The action of Japan at Washington was in part, at any rate, the result of the knowledge Japanese diplomatists had of the situation at home. The leaders of Japan are astute enough to know that they cannot be altogether independent of popular support. There is an increasing and increasingly vocal minority whose opinions are having a slight, though appreciable, effect upon the policy of the country. China's hope of coming to her own in the Far East—the hope, indeed, we all may have of a stable and just peace between these two countries—rests very largely on what this group is able to accomplish in the near future. I believe that we cannot understand the real Japan only by studying her international acts or her internal legislation. We must try to pierce beneath the surface. The whole life and spirit of Japan have been shaken to their depths by the strange and difficult experience through which she has passed in the last half century. What she has done to meet the demand is nothing short of marvellous. She has saved her body politic from disaster. Can she now save her soul? On the answer to this question hangs the fate not only of Japan but also of China and it may be of many another nation. Because I believe in that possibility I am not without hope for the Far East.

CHAPTER VIII

CHINA, EUROPE AND AMERICA

HAVING given Japan a somewhat large share of attention let us come back to China's relations with European nations and with America. We have already seen how these relationships were established and we have traced the stages by which economic imperialism has fastened its hold upon China during the last eighty years since the first opium war. We may just remind ourselves of the following facts :—

1. The ruling factor in the opening of China has been economic—the desire for trade expansion on the part of Western nations.
2. China has not, in the main, welcomed the approaches of these nations.
3. The relationships of China and the West have been vitiated by the fact that these nations were stronger in a military sense, and could insist on their views at the point of the sword or in some other brutal way.
4. China's own weakness, first under an effete foreign dynasty (the Manchus) and later under a form of republicanism not yet well established, has contributed to her exploitation.
5. The concessions wrung from China have been given legal sanction in treaties to which China has often been an unwilling signatory. China has had little reason to suppose that

Western nations really believed in justice, in the broader meaning of the term and where a weak nation was concerned.

6. Nevertheless China has not yet lost all hope of gaining justice through open discussion. She has not yet been driven wholly to abandon the way of patience, persuasion and reasonableness. This is one of the most amazing facts in contemporary history.

In this chapter I want to review the present position of China *vis-à-vis* the nations of the West and I shall do it under the following headings :—(*a*) *General*. 1. Political : extra-territoriality, League of Nations, etc.; 2. Commercial : tariff, new consortium, etc.; 3. Religious ; the missionary movement as a factor in international understanding. (*b*) *Special* : dealing with certain nations specifically.

(*a*) GENERAL.

1. *Political.*—It is recorded that on April 22, 1919, a week or two before the decision on the Shantung question, President Wilson thus addressed the Chinese delegates in the presence of M. Clemenceau and Mr. Lloyd George :—

"As soon as the proposed League of Nations is established, we will give China all our assistance and aid to remove all present inequalities as well as restrictions upon her legitimate rights, so that the Republic of China shall truly become a perfect, independent, sovereign, great State. . . . Such sentiments, I am happy to state, are also shared by Baron Makino, who will likewise be glad to assist in this worthy direction." [1]

During the three and a half years that have elapsed

[1] Quoted by Mr. Tyau in *China Awakened*.

CHINA, EUROPE AND AMERICA 145

since that unexceptionable sentiment was uttered very little has been done to give effect to it. China is still regarded as a partially civilized minor Power so far as diplomatic relationships go. The Western nations send to Peking not ambassadors, but ministers. In spite of the decision arrived at in Washington to enquire into the matter, extra-territoriality persists. An agreement was concluded at the Washington Conference, the Four Power Pact, most vitally touching Chinese interests, and China was not even consulted, much less brought in as a partner. China is still regarded as an outsider, a visitor rather than a nation with equal voice and equal rights. The old diplomacy still exists and is still dominated by the idea of force. A nation which cannot use that language is, so to speak, kept on the doorstep.

There is, of course, another side to the question. China has not succeeded in establishing a stable government, her finances are in confusion, she has not reorganized her judicial system so that foreigners would feel any confidence in being justly dealt with by Chinese courts, she still needs loans from foreign banks. And debtors cannot be choosers. It is confessedly very difficult to make good that promise of President Wilson's, and if steps were taken too hurriedly it is more than likely that the creditor nations would suffer, and that China would therefore fail to get the assistance she herself is asking for. But well-informed Chinese recognize these difficulties, and are not asking for impossibilities. What they do ask for is that they may be let alone and allowed to work out their own problem, even if it should mean passing through a stage of even greater disorganization than at present. They feel, and I think they are right, that the process of reorganization has been retarded and made more difficult by the other members of the family of nations, and that China has never had a fair chance. The circumstances leading to her entry into the war are a notable example of this even in very recent years.

The directions in which China's sovereignty is limited beyond that of other States are summed up by Mr. Bau under the following heads :—

1. Extra-territoriality and consular jurisdiction.
2. Settlements and concessions.
3. Leased territories, such as Kowloon, Port Arthur, etc.
4. Spheres of influence or interest.
5. Limitations due to the working of the Most Favoured Nation Clause, e.g. the inability of China to effect changes in her relations with foreign Powers, without the consent of all.
6. Restrictions in regard to the tariff.

In some of these matters no limitations need be implied if there was reciprocity in the arrangements, as for example in consular jurisdiction, but such reciprocity has not been granted in recent treaties (except those with Germany, Austria and Russia since the war). Some of these matters are co-related so that it would be difficult to change one without involving a change in another. If the system of treaty ports is to be abolished, for example, it could only be done along with a surrender of extra-territorial rights, because consular jurisdiction over any number of people resident far away from a consul with very little effective control and poor means of communication would open the way to grave abuses. While there are certain obvious risks involved in granting to China a complete release from all these galling limitations on her sovereign rights, my own view is that it would be a wise policy to take these risks and to make a somewhat rapid progress towards the complete

CHINA, EUROPE AND AMERICA

removal of them all. I believe that such a policy would help to stimulate China to do her best to justify such a trust, that it would create a new sense of confidence in the goodwill of Western nations; and that it would come nearer than the present state of things to the essential rights of the case.

There is one direction in which a real advance has been made towards the recognition of China's true place in the life of the world. This exception is in the one place where the old diplomacy is giving way before the new, namely, in the League of Nations. While China recognized from the beginning the value of this idea and while she was eager to be a participant in the League, it must not be supposed that Chinese statesmen cherished any illusions in regard to its possibilities. One of her delegates at the Peace Conference, when told that China must look to the League of Nations to redress the Shantung wrong, observed that: (1) "The ruling force in any League constituted at this time will be the same major Powers that composed the Council of Five at Paris and which made the decision in the Shantung question; (2) It is not logical to assume that a League of Nations created by the same body as the Treaty and in conjunction with the Treaty, is designed to reverse the terms of the Treaty; and (3) It is only the so-called weak nations that are asked to depend for justice and security upon the League of Nations, while the so-called Powers openly decline to rest their own positions and security on the League alone and plainly regard its assurance to be insufficient."[1] . . . This may sound rather cynical, but it has been largely borne out by the event and shows the usual shrewdness of the Chinese in seeing through a situation.

China refused to sign the Treaty with Germany because of its inclusion of the Shantung decision,

[1] Quoted by Tyau, op. cit., p. 328.

but was able, nevertheless, to come into the League as a signatory of the Treaty with Austria. Dr. Wellington Koo was elected by the smaller states as one of their representatives on the Council, and on several of the commissions Chinese have done useful work. If the new diplomacy displaces the old, if a new idea of public right takes hold of men's minds in so compelling a way as to exorcise the demon of force and to free men's minds from the fetters that fear has made, then China will come to have an increasing influence in international politics. In fact, one may say that China's influence is already being felt in that direction. The persistent appeal to the public conscience in the Shantung affair has at last won through, and we have an example of what can be achieved, in the face of great obstacles, by a nation that goes on hoping against hope that the justice of her case will make its own appeal at the bar of humanity. In fact, I think it is not too much to say, that we have had a foretaste of the kind of influence which China will increasingly exert as she comes into the family of nations. While politically she is still not fully accepted in the family and while it is difficult to see how she can be so accepted until certain internal changes have been effected, we can see that China already has a peculiar place in the family, even politically, and is doing something which nations usually accounted stronger cannot so effectively do.

2. *Commercial.*—China's own industrial problem must be left over till the next chapter. Here I must deal with her standing as an economic factor in the family of nations. During the last thirty years the foreign trade of China has increased enormously, by something over 500 per cent. It has also changed in certain very interesting directions. Imports and exports have risen together, and China

CHINA, EUROPE AND AMERICA 149

in 1919 exported goods of very nearly as great a value as her imports, that year was, however, an exceptional one in this respect. In the main her exports are raw materials and her imports manufactured goods, but the rapid increase of factories during the last ten or fifteen years has brought about a distinct change in this respect.

In 1879, tea was the chief export, being nearly 50 per cent. of the total, and silk came an easy second with 40 per cent. In 1919, tea had dropped to 4 per cent., silk to 22 per cent., other textiles appear at 10 per cent., and oil-seeds, oil-cakes and vegetable oils take a large place with nearly one quarter of the entire output and a total of about 150,000,000 taels value. Another large item is skins, furs, etc., at about 4 per cent. of the total. This change means also a shifting of the areas of supply and thus of the regions in China of maximum economic prosperity.

In the matter of imports in 1879 nearly one half was opium, and now, so far as the official records are concerned, opium has practically disappeared and tobacco comes up to 4 per cent. In the matter of foodstuffs China is practically self-supporting, as the imports and exports roughly balance. One-third of the imports in 1919 was composed of manufactured cotton goods, a proportion that is likely materially to decrease as Chinese factories are multiplied. Machinery, varied iron goods and hardware occupy a large place in the import schedule. A fact of very great significance is the rapidly increasing place that Japan is taking in the percentage of trade, although, of course, the rate of increase has been materially checked by the persistent boycott during the last few years.

This brief summary will give some idea of the nature of China's place in the economic world. She is a consumer of manufactured goods and of certain raw materials which cannot be obtained locally or in sufficient quantity to meet the demand. Of these latter mineral oils are perhaps the chief. It is certain that China will develop industries which will decrease the demand for certain classes of foreign manufactures. For some, such as machinery, dyes, drugs, etc., which require more highly specialized industries there is likely to be a steadily increasing demand as China becomes more settled and the scale of living rises. One may say at present that Chinese workers live on not more than one-tenth of the income required by a worker in America. If there should be, with the growth of industries and a settled government, a great increase in the prosperity of the country, it is certain that this difference will become less and less. That means that China will buy, for many years to come, very largely indeed from other more industrialized countries. It would not be suprising if Shanghai became the most important trade centre in the world within say fifty or a hundred years. It is the port which gives access to a larger population probably than any other in the world. Its position at the mouth of the Yangtse is extraordinarily favourable, although, of course, many ocean vessels now pass Shanghai and proceed to Hankow or other ports far up the Yangtse. It has already been selected as one of the most favourable sites for factories, as raw materials can easily be delivered there from China or from foreign countries and there is a plentiful supply of cheap labour.

At present Chinese factories cannot turn out much more than supplies the local demand, except in one or two special lines. But there is no doubt that this position is being rapidly changed. Chinese labourers, man for man, when given proper conditions, are not inferior to those of any other country. I was told in Shanghai recently that the delicate work on filaments for electric light bulbs is better done by the Chinese workers than by Americans. This is in a factory where the Chinese are given conditions which compare favourably with those in other countries. When one considers the scale of living and, therefore, the rate of wages, it is easy to see that Chinese manufactures are certain, as they expand, to enter into very keen competition with those of Europe or America. Already American raw cotton is brought to China, spun into yarn and reshipped to America to be made into piece goods to be sold, in many instances, in China. If this double transport is justified by the low cost of labour in China it is certain that the time is coming when Chinese factories will carry the process further, and thus cut out the intermediate process in America. Western nations have made war on China in order to open up a market for their goods. British and other workmen have shed their blood that Chinese people might buy their products and so virtually pay their wages. The time is drawing near when the British worker will be threatened with starvation because the China, opened by his efforts, is underselling him in the home market. The British capitalist who has directed the policy has also been keen enough to see which way the cat would jump. He is in China, in Shanghai and other great cities, there building up the factories which will thrive when the home ones are starved out. Individual capitalists in Britain and other Western nations will, of course, be left in the lurch ; but there are not a few who will be the gainers rather than the losers. The British capital invested in Chinese factories is in some measure an insurance against the time when Chinese industry cuts out British industry, not only in China, but in the markets of the world.

This is a black prospect for the peace of the world.

The British working-man is not likely to take it lying down even if the capitalist has insured himself against loss. There is no knowing what the development of this situation may mean for inter-racial and international relations. It is urgently necessary that this problem should be seen by far-sighted persons on both sides of the world in order that the solution may be sought not in defensive measures, in tariff wars, or in inter-racial conflicts, but in a new spirit in the world family and in the adjustments which good-sense and good-will may be able to devise. Such thoughts as these lead one to look for far-reaching changes in our whole social order and for a far deeper infusion of the Chritian spirit in order that China's fuller entry into the family of nations economically may not spell disaster for humanity. In the next chapter we shall deal with the first of these matters. With the second we must deal in the following section.

Before going on to this point, however, let me touch on two other questions that come under the heading of commercial intercourse. One of the chief ways in which China feels that she is hampered by her foreign connections and the treaties that have been exacted from her at various times is in the matter of the tariff. According to these arrangements China can only make her own tariff within certain very restricted limits. It so works out that she has to accept such a tariff as the nations which trade with her may mutually agree upon. She cannot use her tariff as a means of making any trade bargains with other nations which may erect impassable barriers against her exports. She cannot discriminate between different kinds of imports such as luxuries and necessities, nor can she, where a good chance presents, increase her duties for revenue purposes. The reason advanced by the trading nations is that they need a fixed rate in order to justify large expenditures on setting up a new trade, for such outlay would not be justified if the trade might at any moment be brought to a standstill by an exorbitant tariff. To show how much China is handicapped by lack of tariff autonomy I may mention that, while Japan charges a duty of 355 per cent. on tobacco and carries on a very profitable government monopoly behind the tariff wall, China can only charge a 5 per cent. duty. In regard to spirits, China's duty cannot be more than $4\tfrac{1}{2}$d. a gallon, while we in England charge no less than 15s. 2d. China's demand for a revision of this arrangement seems to me, as I have already said, perfectly reasonable. She asked at Washington to be allowed to raise her tariff from 5 per cent. to $12\tfrac{1}{2}$ per cent. as a first stage, to differentiate between different classes of goods and finally, after a given period, to be granted complete tariff autonomy. The strong interests that might suffer by granting these requests, Japan in particular, have been able so far to prevent more than a very small step being taken ; but a treaty was drawn up at Washington which makes provision for a complete overhauling of the matter and looks to taking a definite step in the direction of tariff autonomy in China. It is too soon to say whether this will be in practice as considerable a step as appears on paper.

There are a few things to be said as to the new Banking Consortium which bear upon our view of the whole situation. This Consortium is the expression of a desire on the part of the powers, and particularly on the part of America, to maintain the open door and to avoid a repetition of the scramble for spheres of influence and special privileges. Japan came in very reluctantly on this basis, as she was most anxious to retain her special position in Manchuria and

154 CHINA IN THE FAMILY OF NATIONS

in Eastern Inner Mongolia. Finally, however, she yielded the point to the persistent pressure of England and America. The Consortium was formed by banking groups in America, England, France and Japan, and each group has the backing of its own government. The ostensible purpose is to help China, to avoid international rivalries, but not to cut out individual enterprise. Loans are to be made for public purposes and for the great public services railways, canals, etc., and are to be given to a responsible Chinese Government under adequate guarantees. The chief dangers that I see in this policy are—

1. That the governments may use default as a means of securing further special privileges and finally a kind of international economic control of China.
2. That the fact that a particular government in China has contracted the loan, may mean that united foreign influence is brought to bear to bolster up that government when the people desire a change, and so there may be again indirectly undue foreign influence in China's internal affairs.
3. That the system of Western capitalism is thereby fixed upon China so that her social order cannot be so developed as to avoid some of the evils of that system. This danger will be more apparent when we deal in the next chapter with China's industrial problem.

On the other hand there are certain real gains :—

1. Japanese exclusive policy in Manchuria and Eastern Inner Mongolia has received a check.
2. The Powers have formally relinquished the idea of spheres of influence.
3. A China that honestly seeks to build up her

economic and political structure has a source from which she can obtain the needed funds without raising international jealousies, etc.

We may say, therefore, in reviewing China's commercial relations with the West that very much hangs in the balance at the moment and that all friends of China should watch developments very carefully and be ready to bring their influence to bear in encouraging right and restraining wrong ones. The next ten years are likely to be fateful ones for China in her economic relations with the rest of the world, but ten years will not nearly see her through her problems in this matter.

3. *Religious Contacts.*—This is not the place to deal at all fully with the manifold work of Christian missions, but there are certain aspects of the work which demand attention if we are to understand the position of China in the family of nations. The contact of missionaries with China has not been in all respects a happy one. Although China is essentially tolerant in matters of religion, she has not always shown herself tolerant towards missionaries from the West. This is due to a variety of causes of which the chief seem to me to be the following:—

(i) The first missionaries came from Western countries which were seeking to press their unwelcome trade upon China. These missionaries were suspected partly because they were unknown and partly because it was assumed that they were agents of trade in another form. They suffered, that is, from the general prejudice against foreigners.

(ii) Roman Catholic missionaries obtained powers similar to those of Chinese officials. These they exercised in a way that was not infrequently very partial to their own converts. Other Chinese joined the Protestant bodies in the hope (not always without foundation) of obtaining support in their legal affairs from Protestant missionaries. Thus missionaries became mixed up in law-suits and many Chinese came to think of them as interfering unjustifiably in purely Chinese affairs.

(iii) Some of the innovations of missionaries in themselves aroused suspicion. Hospitals were supposed to poison patients, orphanages to rob children of their eyes in order to prepare medicines, and so forth. Thus a good deal of suspicion was aroused in the minds of the ignorant, and missionaries, not always careful to observe Chinese etiquette or to study the point of view of those among whom they worked, were the objects of dislike and even of attack.

(iv) In several cases the murder of missionaries was made the occasion of exactions, and in one or two cases of terribly severe exactions, from China. This, though not the fault of the missionaries, gave colour to the identification of the missionary movement with the political ambitions of foreigners.

(v) Missionaries have introduced, along with the simple Christian message, other things which are open to objection. The whole method of work, the buildings erected and the organization formed seemed foreign and gave colour to the idea that missionaries were in China to denationalize her. One very unfortunate step, in my view, has been the introduction of military drill in connection with some schools and colleges, a practice which, when it was introduced, was quite foreign to the Chinese idea of the scholar's life and which seemed to identify the missionary with the military aspect of Western civilization.

While it is only right that we should see in what directions the missionary movement is open to criticism and where its association with other activities has hindered its usefulness, the broad fact remains that this movement is the one considerable avenue of approach to China where Westerners have been inspired by altruistic motives. There may be an element of exploitation even in the missionary movement, that is to say, it is possible for the enthusiastic propagandist to look upon men and women rather as possible converts than as persons, as means to a certain end, such as building up a great organization, rather than as ends in themselves. But this charge cannot be laid against the movement as a whole. The more one sees those who are in it, and the more one knows of the Chinese who have been helped through it, the more thankful one must be that there is one point where the West is sincerely seeking to give its best without thought of gain, where men and money are being devoted not to getting " returns " but to enriching persons in body, mind and spirit. Broadly speaking, the missionary movement is inspired by the thought that the best thing the West has to offer to China is the religion of Jesus Christ, that as this possesses the hearts and lives of Chinese they will be better able to meet their own problems, personal or social, and that in the spirit of Christ unity between East and West can actually be achieved. Pushed as a mere Western propaganda, the missionary movement would be doomed to fail before the rising national spirit. If it meant domination by foreign missionaries or by foreign methods and ideas it would deserve to fail. But what is happening is that Chinese are coming to take the leading places in the Christian movement in China and that the foreigner is, in most cases, gladly stepping aside that this process may continue. No doubt there are cases where the rate at which the change can be made is differently estimated by the two sides, but it does not always happen that the

158 CHINA IN THE FAMILY OF NATIONS

Chinese stand for the more rapid pace. At the great National Christian Conference in May 1922, the suggestion came from the foreigners that a council should be formed consisting entirely of Chinese who might ask missionaries to act as advisory members. It was the clear sentiment of the responsible Chinese leaders that this would be too rapid an advance which led to the formation of a council in which foreigners are full members although in a minority.

It is not possible to say that Christianity has yet fully vindicated its power to unite the peoples of the world or to shape our social and national policies. No nation can be called a Christian nation, and the Western States have certainly not exhibited the Christian virtues in any clear way in their dealings with China. Therefore, we need not wonder if there is still a measure of doubt in the minds of Chinese as to the value of Christianity for their country. But it can be said that many individual Christian Chinese have been trusted by their fellow-citizens, that a large number of Chinese who are not Christians have recognised the ability and honesty of men trained in mission schools, and that the Church in China is one of the chief factors making for social betterment and international goodwill. These statements I should like to support in a little more detail.

(i) *Individual Chinese Christians.*—Among the most trustworthy leaders in China to-day anyone would pick out such persons as the following :—

Dr. W. W. Yen, a third generation Christian, and at one time professor in St. John's University, Shanghai. He has held several of the chief diplomatic posts, has represented his country in America (as Secretary to the Chinese Legation), in Germany and Denmark (as minister), and held office as Foreign Minister from 1920–1922. It was a matter of common knowledge in Peking when I was there that his

CHINA, EUROPE AND AMERICA 159

ministry was one where bribes were not accepted. He was universally admitted to be above suspicion in this matter.

Dr. C. T. Wang, for some time a Y.M.C.A. Secretary and still in close touch with this and other branches of Christian effort. He was vice-Minister of Commerce and Industry in the first Republican Cabinet, twice acted as Vice-President of the Senate, represented the Southern Government at Versailles and was later appointed by the North as well; a signal mark of confidence when the two were in open opposition to one another; was chosen to take over the transfer of the Shantung railway from Japan to China after the Washington Conference, a position needing the most trustworthy personality available, and has held a number of other public posts.

Dr. Chang Po Ling, a Christian man of very high character who has been a leading spirit in educational advance in North China and has founded, among other schools, the Nankai College in Tientsin, a first-rate Chinese college on modern lines, unconnected with any mission and not related to the Church organically but exerting a powerful religious influence.

Dr. S. T. Wen, Commissioner of Foreign Affairs in Nanking, who with *Dr. David Yui*, General Secretary of the Y.M.C.A. for China, was chosen by the Chambers of Commerce and Educational Associations to go to Washington as people's representative, watch the negotiations and give an unofficial report to China. These two men were thus trusted by the whole nation when they could not place the same confidence in government delegates.

All these men I know personally. They are but a few of a goodly number who have gained from Christian education something which has fitted them for public service in a marked degree. When we remember that the Protestant Christians of China

are but one in a thousand in the population it is the
more noteworthy that so many men are coming from
this small group to share in the leadership of the
new China. Speaking of the way in which loans
were obtained from foreign countries, which were to
be spent in arming China to resist the aggressions of
these same countries, I remarked on the curious
paradox. Here is the true armament forged in many
a school and college, worn not on the body, but in
the heart, the creation of men and women whose
character will win respect and confidence, and who
will help China not by leading her away from her
distinctive line of development into the pitfalls of
militarism and materialism; but who will discover
China's true message for the world, who will reinterpret
her deepest aspirations and enable her to meet the
West on the highest plane and in the spirit of brother-
hood. Such persons China needs sorely, and the
West, through her missionary efforts, is helping to
create them, a truly notable contribution to the
solving of the problem of China.

(ii) *The Church and Social Problems.*—The Chinese
Church is only just beginning to express itself, but
already there is a clear evidence that she is not going
to leave the world to go to the devil and calmly save
her own soul. She believes in the Kingdom of God
on earth, not simply as a distant ideal dependent
upon a miraculous visitation, but as that for which
the Church is to work here and now, dependent upon
the degree of her faithfulness to the teaching and
spirit of her founder. In one of the reports for the
National Christian Conference already referred to,
a considerable section is given to an attempt to state
China's present social problem and the Christian line
of approach to it. Recommendations touch
agricultural life, village communities, technical
training, the reorganization of industry, child and

CHINA, EUROPE AND AMERICA 161

women's labour, business morality, care of illiterates and of degenerates, public health, slavery, prostitution and many other aspects of our social disorder. A church that boldly tackles these problems is going to win the confidence of the best people in China. In the message drawn up solely by Chinese men and women we read: "We believe that sin is not only fundamentally an individual problem, but that it is also social. We believe that an unjust economic order, an unrighteous political régime, unfair treatment of any human being, or of any group, is unacceptable to the righteous and loving God." At the conference the one resolution passed besides those looking to the establishment of a permanent council was that which endorsed the International Labour Standard and urged its application to China. Thus at the very beginning of its coming together and speaking out on any matter at all, Chinese Christianity makes it perfectly clear that these questions are of vital interest to it.

(iii) *The Church and International Questions.*—One illustration must suffice to show how Chinese Christians are likely to move in these matters. No question has stirred China more deeply in recent years than the aggressive policy of Japan. I found the country and the Church very deeply moved on this matter. I made it my aim to discuss the question with Christian leaders, and I soon found that it would be possible to bring together a group of Chinese and Japanese Christians to face the issue in a spirit of prayer and mutual goodwill. It was a task not dissimilar to that which some of us attempted during the war—a meeting of Christians of all nations to pray for peace and to talk frankly with one another. It was very hard to get support for such an idea among British Christians. Chinese Christians did not find it easy to think of meeting Japanese. Their feelings had been deeply stirred and they knew their action would be open to criticism. Nevertheless, nearly every one of the leading Chinese with whom I spoke warmly supported the idea, and two such meetings have been held where there was the utmost frankness and yet perfect goodwill and where the Christian spirit triumphed in a truly remarkable way over the spirit of nationalism. There was no running away from the issue or covering it up with sentimental talk. Some speeches were almost brutal in their frankness. There was a determined common effort to discover the truth and to find out how the situation could be dealt with. I am sure the Church in China is going to make itself felt as a factor in the international relations of the country and as a factor that will steadily work for peace based on right relationships.

To sum up then, I see in the Christian movement in China the chief direction in which China's coming into the family of nations is being dealt with in the right spirit. In this sphere she is seeing the West at its highest point in the persons of devoted and large-hearted men and women, she is discovering how she may relate herself to the higher life of the West and how she may give her best to the West in the common enterprise of the Spirit. Those elements in the movement which are open to criticism do not by any means destroy its value. They should certainly be dealt with and removed,[1] and all that tends to genuine Chinese leadership and Chinese thought should be encouraged. In this way Western nations may help China to see that there are some who truly believe in China's own greatness and who seek her presence among the nations not for the profit

---

[1] Anyone who follows missionary movements will realize that this is being done.

CHINA, EUROPE AND AMERICA 163

to be gained from her commerce, but for the enrichment of our common life in the one family.

In a few words I must try to bring out the chief points in the special position of the different Western nations in China. What I have already said refers in a broad way to all, but there are some notable exceptions, especially due to changes that have taken place since the Great War. These we may consider best by treating each nation separately.

America.—When I first went to China in 1905, there was a boycott of American goods in many of the large cities on account of the exclusion of Chinese on the Pacific Coast. The anti-American feeling was quite strong. To-day the feeling towards America is very cordial. I think this due mainly to the following facts :—

(1) America has stood for the open door policy. In spite of what was felt to be the betrayal of China at Versailles for which America was blamed in part, though not so much as other nations, there is a general feeling in China that America means to do the right thing by China. This was strengthened by the Washington Conference, although America's entering into treaty relations with Japan (along with France and England) was criticized.

(2) America has been less aggressive in a military sense than other Western Powers and has never been at war with China, nor sought any territorial expansion at China's expense. It is true that America did join with other nations in the march on Peking after the Boxer outbreak, but her action in that matter was less criticized than that of some other Powers.

(3) The return to China of a large part of the Boxer indemnity has very favourably influenced Chinese opinion. It is said that America claimed

more than her losses, while Britain very carefully estimated her losses and only claimed a fair amount. If this be true America has gained much undeserved *kudos* for her actions, and it is not right to blame Britain for not having followed her example. But in any case American credit has risen immensely through this action and one constantly hears it spoken of.

(4) Partly as a result of this act many more Chinese study in America than in any European country. Thus many returned students favour America, which has certainly on the whole treated Chinese students well. In fact, I have heard the criticism that certain American colleges let down their standards for Chinese. If this is true, I do not think it is any true kindness to China. Certainly there are Chinese who have gained high degrees in America who would not be likely to attain similar distinction in Britain

(5) Americans generally are more approachable than Britishers and seem to have less race prejudice. Whether in the long run their friendship is any truer it is not for me to say, but certainly they have a way with Chinese that often compares favourably with that of my own fellow countrymen.

(6) The large educational work of American Missions and the work and policy (especially in encouraging Chinese leadership) of both the Y.M.C.A. and the Y.W.C.A. has made a great impression. Both these have been started mainly under American leadership, although Britain has a certain share in them. Now they are both led largely by Chinese.

There is no doubt that American policy in China is, like that of other great industrial countries, largely influenced, if not determined, by financial considerations. American business has profited by the wars in which Britain and France opened up China, but America not having shared in them has escaped the

CHINA, EUROPE AND AMERICA 165

odium. In some respects the present good feeling towards America may be rather more than she deserves, if one may use such an expression. Nevertheless, we in this country should take the lesson to heart. It is no use to chafe at the facts. On the contrary we should see that our policy is more deeply influenced by those altruistic ideas which have certainly played a real part in shaping that of America.

Britain.—The feelings towards Great Britain entertained by most Chinese at the present time are certainly much less cordial than those towards America. This is due to the following causes in the main :—

(1) Past history, especially the opium wars and Britain's record in regard to the opium traffic. Her recent action in bringing this traffic to an end can scarcely be said to have neutralized the previous impression.

(2) The Anglo-Japanese Alliance which has led to the conviction that Japan's policy in China had British support and would not have been possible without it.

(3) The comparison made between Britain and America in the matter of the Boxer indemnity.[1]

(4) The way in which Britishers frequently treat Chinese—an attitude of reserve or of condescension rather than of free equal friendship.

On the other hand Chinese recognize that British policy has in certain respects compared favourably with that of other countries. A Chinese writer says : " The policy of Great Britain in China was characterized in a marked degree by justice and fair play."[2] Her action in bringing the opium trade to an end even before the specified time has awakened

[1] Since the above was written this difference has been brought to an end by the action of the British Government. The pity is it was not taken long ago. He gives twice who gives quickly.

[2] Mr. J. Bau, op. cit., p. 142.

favourable comment. Her business men have a high reputation for honesty and for supplying goods up to specification. The work of Sir Robert Hart and a number of other Britishers in the Customs and other public services in China has been greatly appreciated and has done much to enhance British reputation. Her loyal support of the policy of the open door is also of good omen. Sir John Jordan by his friendliness and fairness won his way among all classes in China and was a very real asset. Now that the Anglo-Japanese Alliance has been terminated and the Indo-Chinese opium traffic finally abolished, I think there is a good chance of the British position in China improving. I believe that Chinese and British have very much in common. Both are colonizing and trading peoples, both have a highly developed sense of justice, and are conspicuous for business honesty. In neither do we see so great a development of the sentimental and emotional side of their natures as to outweigh the claims of common sense. The appeal to reason and to the sense of humour carries further than the appeal to mere sentiment. Peace will always, I imagine, be a more alluring ideal to the bulk of Chinese than military glory, and I think the same is true of Britons. If I am right in this opinion it seems a natural conclusion that Britain and China between them may do a very great work for humanity, and that close friendship and mutual understanding is not only desirable, but easily realizable. If Britain, America and China could stand together for peace and righteousness in the world during the next century they would have an untold influence in controlling and modifying the war policies of more volatile and more imperialstic people.[1] Much

---

[1] I do not want this to be understood as suggesting a close alliance, rather common effort, in which I should hope that other nations would share.

depends on Britain following a truly democratic path in dealing with the great nations she is now governing. Her action in India is closely watched in China. She must vindicate her belief in the rights of other nations by her action in her own Empire, if she is to inspire the confidence of democratic Chinese. Given this, and a policy of persistent friendliness to China, there is no reason why Britain should be any less trusted and respected in China than is America. These three countries in unity would mean the unity of more than half the world's inhabitants. Such unity would make for peaceful development and for a steady widening of the area of democratic control in industry as well as in politics without violent upheavals and their consequent reactions.

France.—Not having travelled in the parts of China chiefly under French influence, I cannot speak much at first hand of the position of France in China. As far as my information and observation goes, I should say there was a good deal of suspicion of French policy. Her alliance with Imperialist Russia, and her policy of aggression in the South, have been open to strong criticism. More recently her rapprochement with Japan and the feeling that she is following an imperialist and militarist line in world affairs have brought her under sharp criticism. As France has joined with Britain and the United States in the new Banking Consortium and is thus committed to the generally favourable policy and the open door, there seems to be a disposition to hope that French policy, along with British, will become more helpful in the future. The fact that the Roman Catholic missionaries are largely French and under French protection has had a double effect. In regard to the large Roman Catholic population (about two million) and many others benefited by the work, it produces friendly feeling. Outside this area there is antagonism due to the special privileges and status claimed by the priests in the past and their interference in law cases. These privileges having been withdrawn this difficulty is largely removed. The French have established a Government hospital in Chengtu which does good work, and in one or two other ways have shown their desire to help China. Unfortunately, an ambitious scheme for Chinese students to come over to France for combined work and study, which was much appreciated when first adumbrated, has broken down. Many students were reduced to penury in a strange land, and there has been a consequent revulsion in Chinese minds.

Germany.—I think no European nation is more popular in China to-day than is Germany. This may seem strange when one remembers German aggression in Shantung and the fact that Germany and China have been on opposite sides in the Great War. It is due in part to the fact that Germany has been treated by her conquerors in a way that makes China feel a deep sympathy, a sort of fellow-feeling. China and Germany were both wronged by the Treaty of Versailles, both are suffering because might has overstepped the bounds of right. Chinese recognize that the Germany of to-day is not the Germany that arrogantly demanded the concessions in Shantung. Again, new treaties with Germany have removed her special privileges, and her concessions in Tientsin and Hankow have reverted to Chinese control. The Boxer indemnity was also cancelled as a result of China's coming into the war. This means that Germans are now in China on equal terms with Chinese. Even though the change has not been of Germany's seeking, it has helped greatly in the reaction of feeling. German merchants are offering their goods on very favourable terms with long credits, and the low valuta enabled them at one

CHINA, EUROPE AND AMERICA 169

time to sell at a lower price than England or America. Probably this has been changed since I left China in the summer of 1922 by the very rapid fall of the mark. The very fact that there is still a great deal of anti-German prejudice among foreign merchants in China tends rather to cause Chinese to look favourably upon Germans. Their strong sense of justice is awakened and they incline to side with the " bottom dog." It is a question whether the gains which have come to Germany through the surrender of extra-territoriality and other privileges may not in the long run outweigh the losses.

Russia.—Twenty years ago Russia was the most feared of all the European nations. Her steady encroachment on China right up to the gates of Peking, her uncanny power of seeming a friend, while acting as an enemy, had aroused a deep resentment and distrust. Soviet Russia has abandoned this policy. Russians have now no special privileges. Many Russians are destitute and depend upon charity. China sees in Russia another country suffering at the hands of militaristic and capitalistic nations and making a daring experiment in a new form of government. It is surprising to find how Bolshevik ideas have spread among young Chinese not mainly because of the methods of violence used, but because Young China sees in Russia a bold attempt to throw off an outworn system and to break with traditions that have hampered her progress. China is in many ways similar to Russia. She has a largely peasant population, poorly developed industries and resources, and a people but little touched as yet by modern education. Is Russia blazing a trail that China, in her own way, may follow ? Such is the question that students and thinkers all over China were asking when I went out at the end of 1920. While in China I noticed a certain change which came from a fuller knowledge of the Russian experiment and from further consideration of the problem. The more thoughtful leaders seemed to be turning away from Bolshevik ideas, fearing the violence and extremes for a people like China, while still much attracted by the original communistic idea. Capitalism is very generally criticized by the Chinese democrats and no considerable experiment in any other way of modern industrial development has been made in the world. This gives Russia a certain standing in the eyes of Chinese and creates what can only be called a glamour that tends to make a true judgment difficult. My own view is that the good sense of China will increasingly turn away from the Russian model as far as method is concerned, but that Chinese thinkers will be constantly using the measure both of success and of failure in Russia as a guide for their own country in facing a problem in some ways strikingly similar to that of Russia. To this question we must return in the next chapter as we consider the industrial situation in China.

CHAPTER IX

THE INDUSTRIALIZATION OF CHINA

WE have reminded ourselves of the very rapid growth of foreign trade in China, of the consequent development of Chinese industry and the effect of these changes in the relations of China with the rest of the world. We have now to consider the consequent changes in China's social structure and in the common life of her people, and to estimate the effect of these changes in her future development.

In some respects the changes in China are similar to those with which all students of the industrial revolution in Europe are perfectly familiar. The movement from the land into large centres of production has begun ; home industries and open-air occupations are giving place to factory life with the consequent effects on health ; there is a tendency for certain crafts to die out and for the joy of individual creation to be lost ; a large wage-earning community is growing up and gradually becoming class-conscious with the consequent dangers of class-war ; the scale of living is rapidly increasing with little if any increase in the joy of life. These and similar changes, taking place at a rate far greater than in most other countries and with the additional irritant of their being caused by foreign interference in a country where change has been almost unknown, are producing results the full effect of which it is very difficult to estimate or forecast. My object is to present them in such a way as provide a starting point for further study as the drama unfolds itself. A necessary preliminary is a brief survey of China's original social and industrial life.

The problems that China is facing to-day can never be understood unless it is always remembered that the family is the social, the industrial and the political unit. The family is of the patriarchal type, including in one home several generations, for the sons bring their wives back to live in the family homestead and do not, as a rule, set up their own home. The place of the family in Chinese life is something which a Westerner only gradually comes to understand and appreciate. In fact, it may be said that no Westerner can fully understand it. Within the family circle we have a miniature kingdom, a self-contained community under an autocracy more or less benevolent and a kind of communism in practice though not in theory. While in many things, the father is an autocrat and a pretty stern one at that, and while, in domestic matters, the position of the mother is also very autocratic, there is a certain sense of mutual relationship and responsibility that frequently surprises the outsider. The interests of the family are one. If one member suffers, all suffer with him, even in extreme cases sharing his punishment when he comes under the law, and often making good his defalcations when he has committed a crime. In the success of one member all share, and what we would describe as wanton nepotism, is, in China, a perfectly natural expression of the family spirit. Not to bring a share of one's prosperity to one's near relations would be the most unnatural kind of conduct. There are many codes of family laws in China which date back for thousands of years. They cover the widest

THE INDUSTRIALIZATION OF CHINA 173

ranges of conduct. They are not stereotyped in any final form, and different families have their own unwritten rules which are binding upon all members. Disputes between members of the family are almost invariably settled within the family,[1] and disputes between one family and another involve the whole connection on either side. The ancient social system which rested upon the grouping of a hundred families with one head man, and with a sense of mutual responsibility throughout the group for any member, may be taken as an illustration of the way in which Chinese social organization is based on family solidarity, with its ultimate sanction in the time-honoured custom of ancestor-worship. As one Chinese puts it: "Although the lot of a Chinese, whether a parent or a son, seems so surprisingly hard, and the rising generation, imbued with the so-called advanced ideas, resents the old idea of supporting the whole family, it may be said that the old system—that is, family socialism—is, on the whole, socially desirable. Under such a system the whole population may be equally poor, but they are, I conceive it, better than the community in which many are deprived even of bare subsistence, while others enjoy a fortune of millions."[2]

In The Great Learning we have this statement of the position of the family: "The tranquillity and happiness of the world depends on rightly governed states. A rightly governed state necessitates well-regulated families. A well-regulated family is made possible only by the self-culture of the individuals comprising it." Thus we see that social theory in China introduces the family between the State and the individual. The question naturally arises in

---

[1] The Chinese proverb says: "Even a clever magistrate can hardly arbitrate family matters."
[2] L. K. Tao, in *Village and Town Life in China*.

our minds as to whether manhood suffrage is China's true method of democracy, and whether it may not be possible to work out a political system resting on the conception of family unity. The difficulty is that modern industrial developments and Western ideas of personal liberty are combining to cut out the middle term as an effective force in the life of the people. This is one of the most fundamental aspects of the present situation in China.

Another ancient part of Chinese social life is the system of guilds or co-operative associations. The two chief kinds of guild are the provincial guild and the trade guild. Both are primarily concerned with the industrial organization of the country. In the absence of any strong central government making laws for trade, these guilds have come to take a most important place in Chinese industrial life. The Hwei-kuan (provincial guild) binds together merchants and others who have come from any one province (or in some cases from any one town), and who are residing in another province (or town). These guilds are open to all reputable men from the particular area and such persons are expected to join them. They exist to protect the interests of these "foreigners," and in particular their trade interests. They give benefits to members in special need, help new arrivals, defend their members in law-suits (if they are thought to have a good case); levy a tax upon the members for such common purposes. Their organization is essentially democratic,[1] though the paid secretary comes to have a very large influence in their affairs. They are open both to rich merchants and to ordinary working-men or clerks. These guilds have repeatedly used their influence on behalf of their members to

[1] For example, in many cases the governing body chosen by vote changes its membership annually, so that all come in course of time to serve on it.

THE INDUSTRIALIZATION OF CHINA

secure redress of grievances and generally to further their interests. The Government has to reckon with them on occasion, and they often call on the help of officials who come from the same place as the guild members. They are another example of the great influence of the clan-spirit in Chinese social life.

The trade guilds are much nearer in type to the craft guilds in Europe in the Middle Ages. They are self-governing democracies in which disputes between the members are settled according to the guild's own rules, and where punishments range from small fines to the last terrible weapon of the economic boycott. So powerful are they that no merchant carrying on a particular kind of business can possibly afford to stand outside his trade guild. The guild does not pay much attention to the law of the land, and in all trade matters it makes its own rules, which are rigidly enforced. If a guild member goes to law without first trying every possible resource within his guild and without finally obtaining its permission, he is liable to severe penalties. Trade customs, prices, discount rates, setting up of new business and many other similar matters are controlled by the guild. In fact, it may be said that, while there are many differences between the various guilds, all of them claim the absolute obedience of their members, all regulate in great detail the particular trade or craft, and all are democratic in constitution. They have been for generations the one effective check on dishonesty, unlimited competition and any practice that would bring discredit on the trade, or suffering to those engaged in it. They also control the rules for apprenticeship and so are able to limit the number of persons learning any craft and save the dangers of over-production. They have in them immense possibilities both of good and of ill. They may be the means of serving the community and saving the people from exploitation, or of enriching their own members at the expense of the community.

Turning from these forms of social and industrial organization, let us look for a moment at the industry of China as carried on for thousands of years. Of course the vast majority of the Chinese are in some way connected with work on the land. The agriculture of China is a high art, and intensive cultivation has been developed to such an extent that her huge population, cultivating by no means all the land (only about 15 per cent. of the area of China's twenty-two provinces is now under cultivation), is practically self-sustaining. The people are very largely peasant proprietors, and an immense number of the holdings are quite small ones. In 1917, a land survey showed that of about fifty-eight million holdings over half were of less than thirty mow ($6\frac{1}{2}$ mow to the acre), and less than three millions were over a hundred mow in size. Taking China as a whole far more than half the families living on the land own their own or part of their own farms, although in some provinces, such as Hupeh, the number who rent their farms is a very considerable proportion of the whole, say about one-third. The patriarchal family system means that in most cases the cultivation of any farm lands can be undertaken by the members of the family, and there is comparatively little hired labour. Very often there will be some additional home industry, the keeping of silk-worms, spinning and weaving, a salt-well on the farm, embroidery, or what not. In the busy seasons all hands can be turned to the harvesting or other farm work. In the off-season the home industry occupies the spare time. The family usually does its own marketing, but there is co-operation in special services such as watching the crops as they ripen.

THE INDUSTRIALIZATION OF CHINA

In the smaller and also in the larger towns there are many small industries, frequently carried on in the premises of which the front part is used as a shop for the sale of the produce. The manufacture of toys, leather goods, maccaroni, sweetmeats, paper money, hats and innumerable other articles, embroidery, spinning, mat-making, and indeed almost every form of productive activity, save those processes which need a large plant and special conditions, may be seen as one passes along almost any Chinese street. Even if not immediately visible, they may be discovered by peering behind a door or curtain. In these small industries there may be a certain number of hired persons, and apprentices are frequently taken in and trained. The relations are often cordial and the apprentices come to have a deep sense of loyalty to their master, who in turn helps them when they start on their own. The best of such industries are like large families. The conditions are not what we should call good; often there is overcrowding and the pay may be poor. But the work is done either in fresh air, the whole side of the building being open to street or court-yard, or at any rate in houses so built that neither air nor rain are rigidly excluded ! In many cases there is a system of profit-sharing which may considerably augment the scanty pay. In one case that I know of, the proceeds are divided at the end of three years so that the owner gets four-sixths, the manager one-sixth and the employees one-sixth.

In addition to these small industries, employing rarely as many as a hundred workers, there are a few really big industrial undertakings in China where large numbers of workers have been congregated in a single centre for large-scale production. These concerns are usually due to special circumstances, as in the china factories at Ching-teh-chen,[1] or the salt-

[1] Spelled on some maps King-teh-Chen or Chang-nan-chen.

wells at Tzi-Liu Chin, in Szechwan, where in each case hundreds of thousands of Chinese are working in one place because the materials are at hand. Such industries have been quite the exception in China until the last fifty years or so when the introduction of machinery from the West has caused the aggregation of large numbers of workers in certain centres, chiefly treaty ports.

Women and children share in the work both on the fields and in the home industries or small household factories. Their hours are frequently long, but, when in the open air, this may not be incompatible with healthy growth, as long as the kind of labour is not arduous. The Chinese are a happy, contented people on the whole, and one does not get the impression of much revolt against the evils of this industrial system. The community is fairly homogeneous, owing largely to the family system and the relatively small number of wage-earners, and also, in part, to the absence of any strong sense of social caste. Of course there are good families in China with wealth and education, and others that are poor, illiterate and apparently without the finer traditions and instincts. But the family system has served to make possible the education of one or more members from almost any family if a child showed promise, and not a few of China's great leaders have sprung from the humblest homes. Culture is often present in a high degree in homes where the living is of the simplest and where there is no appearance of wealth or even of comfort. It is this homogeneous society with its close-knit family system, its trade guilds, its home industries, its countless farmsteads, with their small family holdings, which is to-day threatened with disruption by the sudden avalanche of Western industrialism.

It is perfectly clear that Western industrial methods

THE INDUSTRIALIZATION OF CHINA 179

have come to China to stay. No one can put back the hands of the clock and few would wish to do so. There is no movement in China comparable to Gandhi's call away from the factory and back to the hand-loom. Nor is it likely that any such call will be made in China or would find, if made, any considerable response, both because Chinese see the very obvious material advantages of machinery and because there is no added motive, as in India, of shaking off a foreign yoke. The problem then is rather one of directing this new force in ways that will bring the maximum of good with the minimum of loss. With this thought in one's mind we may review some aspects of the changes now taking place.

The largest advance has perhaps been made in improving the means of communication. All parts of China are now connected by telegraph. The postal system is peculiarly good except where, on occasion, brigand bands raid the mails. The steamboat service up the Yangtse (now extended through the gorges to Chung King and above), and on other rivers, is second to none in the world. Railway construction has made very rapid strides, although recently held back as a consequence of internal unrest and the difficulty of raising capital during and since the Great War. Beginning with the Woosung Railway in 1876, built by foreign capital, redeemed by China and then torn up and sent as separate rails to Formosa, the railways have multiplied in China to such an extent that there are now some six thousand kilometres in operation, carrying nearly thirty million persons a year and over twenty million tons of merchandise. This not only greatly facilitates commerce, but it is one of the chief factors making for the change in China's social system, involving a much greater facility of movement than formerly, a rapid spread of new ideas and an inevitable tendency to weaken the home ties. So far as their influence on creating a capitalist class is concerned, the railways may not prove to be a very important factor, although it is true in some cases individual Chinese have very large blocks of capital invested in certain railways. The policy of the Government is being steadily directed towards state ownership, and as the national finances improve I expect this policy to be carried through completely. Already over seventy thousand persons are employed on the railways and in these employees you have one of the large bodies of labourers with common interests whose presence makes for a class-conscious proletariat.

China's mineral resources are being opened up far more fully than ever before in her long history. This is partly due to the break down of the superstition that mining beneath the earth's surface would in many cases bring ill-luck. But it is chiefly the result of the introduction of better methods of prospecting and mining, and to the increase in transportation facilities. The effect of the last-named point may be illustrated from an example in the field of agriculture. In the Wei Basin in Shensi, wheat sells at one-third of the price in Hankow, six hundred miles away, but it is so costly to bring it 300 miles to the railway that even with this difference it cannot be profitably brought to the Hankow market. Wheat can be brought to Hankow from Seattle, nearly seven thousand miles, for half what it costs to bring it six hundred miles from the Wei Basin. This will make clear why mining operations. until the introduction of modern transport facilities, have been often unprofitable.

The resources of coal and iron in China have been greatly exaggerated by some Western authorities. Nevertheless they are very considerable and are in

THE INDUSTRIALIZATION OF CHINA 181

excess of those known to exist in other lands bordering on the Pacific, except America. The most reliable estimate is that made by Mr. Ting, director of the geological survey of China. Coal he puts at between forty and fifty billion tons, about one-third of Britain's resources. Iron ore he puts at fully one thousand million tons, or nearly as much as that of Britain and one-fourth that of the United States. It is perfectly clear that a country with such resources and with other very valuable ores (China has, for example, one half of the world's known resources in antimony) has a great industrial future. The mines of China are being opened up as capitalist enterprises on similar lines to those in other countries, and it is difficult to see how any other method of development would have been possible or could even now be pursued. Large amounts of capital had to be invested in prospecting and in work which was for some time unremunerative. Large risks had to be taken. There was no organization, either of the workers or in local or national government, able in the smallest degree to carry out these operations. In a number of cases foreign capital has been used involving various degrees of foreign control and the use of the output in foreign countries. This is particularly true of the opening of mines under Japanese control during the last fifteen years, particularly in Manchuria. The information that I possess in regard to conditions in the mining districts is not in most cases reassuring. There is, however, one notable exception and it may be well to quote this. It shows what is possible and what may be done elsewhere, as Chinese and other mine-owners awake to the dangers of following a less enlightened policy, or to the advantages of a similar one both to themselves and their employees and to the social progress of China generally. The example I refer to is in the area mined by the

Hanyehping Company (who own the Hanyang Ironworks). An eye-witness so described it in June 1918:—

"A township is being built which in every sense of the word may be considered 'Model.' No difficulty is too great, and no expense is being spared to insure that the workpeople will be well housed and cared for, both mentally and physically. . . . The houses are built on modern European lines with plenty of room, light and fresh air . . . fitted with electric light, for which the company intend making a nominal charge. . . . The company have built, equipped, and placed at the disposal of their employees a magnificent club house, where there will be provided all kinds of indoor and outdoor games and recreation; also a library, reading-room and accommodation for residents."[1]

Unfortunately I have no recent information about this experiment, but I do know that a similar one, the so-called Model City of Nan Tung Chow near Shanghai, has been designed, built and maintained by Chinese, and is a very fine example of what can be done even in a country where standards of living are admittedly very low and where there is much inertia and prejudice to overcome. The hope of China's mining developments being carried through without serious social upheavals seems to rest largely on the far-sightedness and goodwill of the individuals and companies, who have drawn together large numbers of men to work for them in the mines. I see no immediate prospect of the nationalization of mines in China, and it is difficult to see how fresh mining properties can be rapidly opened up without the further use of foreign capital and direction, although, if a slower pace were maintained, it might be possible for Chinese to do this work themselves.

[1] *China Awakened*, p. 223.

THE INDUSTRIALIZATION OF CHINA 183

Turning to the related question of the building of modern factories in China, we find that the problem becomes even more acute. Scarcely anything impressed me more after an absence of over ten years from China than the phenomenal increase in the number and size of modern factories. There is a list of factories in China given in the China Year Book which the publishers specially describe as incomplete. It occupies some twenty-eight pages of that volume with, say, forty or fifty factories on each page. The goods manufactured include albumen, cement, chemicals, cotton, spirits, glass, leather goods, matches, paper, rope, silk, soap, woollens and numbers of other articles of common use. Power plants, flour mills, saw-mills, oil mills, dockyards, iron works and other types of industrial enterprise are included. These factories are nearly all run on foreign or semi-foreign lines, some under foreign and very many under Chinese management. In them, larger or smaller numbers of men, women and children are brought together as wage earners, mainly in the large towns. In many cases there are prodigiously long hours, the twelve-hour day being very usual and the fourteen-hour day not unknown. The problem created is one of the most thorny in the world to-day. There are many local conditions which combine to make it easy to exploit the labourer and difficult for those who would do otherwise. Until lately there has been very little general knowledge of what was happening. Public opinion is difficult to rouse in China, and there has been no education of the public conscience to enable it to appreciate the nature of the evils and risks. Labour has been very plentiful and very cheap. The people have been accustomed to long hours on their fields and do not realize that the same hours in a factory are a very different proposition. Until recently there has been no movement of organized labour to draw attention to the evils and to press for remedies. Even now such movements as exist have little force and are not organized on a national scale. There has been no strong central government to watch developments, to make suitable factory laws or to see that they were observed. If such laws were made in the foreign concessions there was a belief that they would act unfavourably towards factories established there as compared to those outside, and so drive away trade, whereas if similar laws were made by the Government of China or by the local officials, foreign merchants would have little confidence (in the present state of things) in their being enforced. I found a tendency among Chinese employers to blame the foreigner who, they said, cared less for the lives and the health of the Chinese labourer than did their fellow-countrymen. At the same time I am bound to say that I could not detect any truths in this charge. Some of the best factories are under foreign management and some of the worst under Chinese. But the same statement might also be made the other way round. The fact is that there are some individuals, both Chinese and foreign, deeply concerned at the trend of events; but these are the exception, and they find it intensely hard to act alone in ways that they believe would penalize them in the economic struggle. Where experiments of a better type have been made, however, the result has not really been penalization. There has been improvement of work, and better relations between employer and employed have been established. To illustrate the kind of conditions that need remedy let me quote a single case taken from a trade journal about a Shanghai mill.[1]

"The profits of the . . . Cotton-spinning factory again surpassed $1,000,000. To those who bestow

[1] Quoted in *The Christian Revolution*

thought on the progress of textile industries in China, the following particulars regarding this concern may be of interest. The company was started in 1904 with a paid-up capital of $600,000 divided into 6,000 shares of $100 each. The capital was increased to $900,000 in 1916. For the past two years it has been running day and night with scarcely any intermission. The number of hands employed is 2,500, and the following is the wage table per day:

	Minimum Cents. (Mex.)	Maximum Cents. (Mex.)
SKILLED LABOUR (e.g. FOREMEN)—		
Men	35	60
Women	30	50
ORDINARY LABOUR—		
Men	30	50
Women	20	30
Boys (aged about 15)	20	30
Girls (aged about 15)	10	20
Small boys (aged about 10)	10	20
Small girls (aged about 10)	7	10

The working hours are from 5.30 a.m. to 5.30 p.m. and from 5.30 p.m. to 5.30 a.m., respectively. No meals are supplied by the factory. Most of the cotton used is produced locally, and the factory is able to turn out about 7,000 piculs monthly of coarse yarn, chiefly No. 10. It will be seen that the company is in an exceptionally favourable position. With the raw material at their doors, an abundant and absurdly cheap labour supply to draw on, and no vexatious factory laws to observe, it is not surprising that their annual profits have exceeded their total capital on at least three occasions."

In this case it is easy to see that there is immense room for improvement and a margin on which to work without endangering reasonable profits. Unless something is done by firms in such a position as this one it seems certain that labour unrest will develop very greatly. Speaking of child labour, Miss Agatha Harrison, who is now studying the whole problem in Shanghai, writes :—

"This is the most tragic and humiliating sight. It is not easy to generalize on the age when children begin work; many of them are brought in as babies by their mothers. In some of the factories visited women were working with babies strapped on their backs (in one case a woman had her baby strapped in front in order to feed it), and at the same time work with both hands and a foot. Brought up in the factory atmosphere, children learn to do odd jobs at a very early age, and at the ages of six, seven and eight years are to be seen on regular work.

"It is often argued that these little children do not work, but are brought by their mothers who cannot leave them at home. To a certain extent this is true, but the remark of an employer is a significant answer: 'If we stop employing children our mills would have to close down.' Another has said: 'Children's hands are peculiarly well-fitted for this work.' Twelve hours a day, and alternate weeks, twelve hours a night, tell the life history of many little people in China whose heritage the world over is a few years at least of school and play."[1]

Much more could be said on this subject, but enough has been given to make clear the nature of the problem we have to consider. We must now turn from the bare facts of this vast industrial development to consider its deeper significance and its larger results.

The external effect upon the country life of China is two-fold. In the first place there is the usual tendency to draw people from the country to the towns. While this is important, it is at present a

[1] *The Christian Occupation of China*, p. 26.

relatively small factor in the economic life of the country. The population is so vast and there are so many parts of China which are somewhat overpopulated and from which there has been a more or less steady stream of emigration, that so far there has been no serious effect upon the agricultural prosperity upon which China has always depended for her economic stability. This result can hardly fail to figure more largely in the future, and there is likely to be a steady rise of food prices and some shortage in staple products as a more or less recurring symptom of industrial development. On the other hand there is a steady demand for improvement of agricultural produce due to the starting of modern large-scale production and the competition with foreign manufactures. This is seen in the setting up of research stations and considerable efforts in improving the strains of cotton, in weeding out the diseased silk-worms and in attention to the breeding of cattle. These are some of the questions already receiving attention. Many others, such as the combating of anthrax on the Manchurian and Mongolian plains and the breeding of sheep whose wool has a better staple, the improvement of many other crops, re-afforestation and so forth, will receive increasing attention as it becomes clear that the market demands better produce from the country. There is also much room for advance in methods of assembling goods for wholesale shipment, and other co-operative measures.

Far more important, from our point of view, is the inward change in the social structure that is taking place slowly in many places, but rapidly in others. " Modern industry cuts the workers off from their old life with its social ties, its economic inter-relations, and its moral sanctions, and casts them adrift on the currents of an uncharted and troubled sea. China has hitherto shown the most remarkable social stability. Her family and clan system, with the democratic village based upon it, has persisted for four thousand years, surviving repeated foreign conquests of the country. And these families have had an economic stability based on their ownership of the land. What industry and trade there has been, has organized itself in guilds. But the large scale modern industry is growing up entirely outside the guilds, and it is causing the family system to crumble and destroying the almost universal connection with the land—the break with the past is complete. The old supports have largely gone; the old loyalties by which they were upheld, the precepts by which they were guided are disappearing or losing their hold in changed conditions. How are the illiterate, apathetic workers to build up a new social heritage to replace the old?"

So writes Professor Taylor of Peking,[1] and although in one or two particulars I think this statement goes a little far, if meant to apply to the whole of China, it undoubtedly represents the very strong tendency in many parts of the country and what has already happened in some few places. New forms of organization are being erected to take the place of the old, and these forms tend to approximate to Western ideas and thus to involve a break with China's own past, a departure from her *Tao*, or inner nature. Chief among these new forms are the labour organizations springing up in all the industrial centres. These have been strongest in the South and in Eastern Central China as was only natural, both because of the character and traditions of the people and because these are the areas most deeply influenced by foreign commercial enterprises. In Dr. Sun Yat Sen's volume

[1] From an article quoted in *The Christian Occupation of China*, p. 26.

on the *International Development of China*, he pleads for a development of China on socialist lines by foreign capital, largely with the object of avoiding a class-struggle. He sees, as all far-seeing men must, that, unless something be done to prevent it, China is very likely to become the cock-pit for a commercial and a class struggle of extraordinary intensity and bitterness. There are those who assume that the Chinese with their proverbial patience, adaptability and peaceableness, can be exploited almost indefinitely, and that they will not turn against the exploiter. It may also be admitted that capitalists have a tremendous advantage in China, coming with their experience of the class-war and the power of organized labour in other lands to a people ignorant of these things, and with no experience of the methods of industrial development used elsewhere. These considerations justify one in believing that the natural reaction against the capitalist system in China might be long delayed even if there should be much exploitation of Chinese labourers. In the West the growth of labour organizations has greatly checked such exploitation; and unscrupulous capitalists, often banding themselves together for the purpose, have exploited the consumer instead, for in many cases, with the watering of capital and other methods, such exploitation is necessary if even a small return is to be made to the ordinary shareholder. In China both kinds of exploitation can be carried on concurrently, and hence the 100 per cent. profits in such cases as that given a few pages back.

Such a state of things cannot continue. One's first thought as to the means of improving conditions would naturally be to strengthen the labour organizations so that they may effectively operate towards improved conditions of labour, and no doubt this in itself is desirable from many points of view and should have a certain salutary influence. Already a good many strikes have taken place in China and in not a few cases very deplorable conditions have been removed or improved. This method of continual sub-acute warfare between employer and employed, with occasional lapses into open battle, is not, however, a very satisfactory one for true and harmonious progress anywhere, and it is clear to my mind that it is not the method most suited to China, and is really contrary to her national genius.

While Bolshevism has had a certain vogue among Chinese social theorists and students, it seems clear that the good sense of China is revolted by much which is associated with that term. A recent Chinese writer has thus analysed the situation:—

"The idea of a Soviet Revolution in China will quickly evaporate in the light of greater understanding of socio-economic conditions in the Republic. To begin with, the bulk of this nation, even under the Manchus, was never so downtrodden as the Russians under the Romanoffs or the French under the Bourbons, and cut-throat animosity between different classes in conspicuous by its absence. . . . Chinese society is constructed on a horizontal foundation, unlike the vertical stratification of India. . . . 'Down with the bourgeois,' cried the insensate destroyer, but there is no room in this land of horizontal stratification for any vertical distinction between [proletariat], bourgeoisie and aristocracy."[1]

Admitting that "anything may happen," with the growth of modern industry and with the entirely new conditions so created, I should myself be much surprised if any big, violent movement of social revolution developed in China. Nevertheless, there are many of the elements that have contributed to this end in other lands, and the changes which have

[1] Mr. Tyau in *China Awakened*, pp. 235–6.

already taken place warn one against too confident a forecasting of the future. This much is clear that the situation is one which cannot be allowed to drift.

Dr. Sun, in the work already referred to, makes the interesting suggestion that foreign capital should be advanced in such a way as to build up a system of State socialism. He points out that China's backwardness in industrial development is a blessing in disguise (not perhaps a very complete disguise either), and that as a late comer into the field she may be able to gain much from experience in other countries. He says :—" The goal of material civilization is not private profit but public profit. And the shortest route to it is not competition, but co-operation. In my International Development Scheme, I propose that the profits of this industrial development should go first to pay the interest and principal of foreign capital invested in it ; second to give high wages to labour ; and third to improve or extend the machinery of production. Besides these provisions the rest of the profit should go to the public in the form of reduced forces in all commodities and public services. Thus all will enjoy in the same degree the fruits of modern civilization. . . In a nutshell, it is my idea to make capitalism create socialism in China, so that these two economic forces of human evolution will work side by side in future civilization." [1]

While we may think this dream rather too daring it is at least significant as coming from one of the most creative minds in China, and it is not without significance that foreign capital, under the plan of the new International Consortium, is to be available particularly for the development of national enterprises such as railways and canals, under Government management. Is this a first step whereby capitalism is being asked to create socialism ?

[1] Op. cit., pp. 164–5.

My own thinking in regard to the industrial development of China has taken a somewhat different line. I very much doubt whether a centralized scheme of the kind proposed by Dr. Sun is really true to China's own past, and suitable for more than a small part of her industrial development. While I recognize the grave difficulties in the way and while I am far from sanguine as to the possibility in the near future of directing the industrial development of China into any new direction, I believe that attention should be earnestly directed to the problem of the adaptation of China's own industrial machinery to meet the entirely new situation. At present the guild system is breaking down, perhaps, in much the same way as the guilds of the Middle Ages broke down in Europe. The new conditions have come so suddenly as to make adaptations almost impossible ; foreign influence has not been helpful, and there is likely to be a demand for central legislation to take the place of the local and specialized legislation of the trade guilds. In some directions such central legislation will be good, as for example, in securing minimum conditions on such lines as the international standards. But there is much to be said for leaving a large measure of liberty to special trade guilds, especially if these could be so developed as to include *all* who are engaged in an industry, and so make for a form of industrial democracy on a voluntary basis. With this suggestion I would couple the idea that the system of profit-sharing which obtains in a number of small factories in China of the old type should be retained in some form. The Chinese social system seems much more suited to the development of comparatively small factories where all who work together share a common life and can cultivate the idea of common purpose, than to the huge factories where thousands are employed by a limited company which tends to

THE INDUSTRIALIZATION OF CHINA

become impersonal in its activities. Can the new Chinese factories become, as it were, glorified families, where something of the family spirit is carried over into the larger community ? Can China avoid that type of impersonal relationship between employer and employed which is one of the chief causes of the class-war ? I believe there is such a possibility. I have had the vision of China working out her own plan of industrial self-government, in which all those engaged in any factory will be united in a sort of family bond, where there will not be a large body of absentee shareholders who make an unlimited demand on the profits, however limited their liability may be, and where such industrial communities will be united in guilds, locally, provincially, and nationally, making many of their own regulations to secure a high grade of work, good conditions for the workers, the high standard of rectitude for which Chinese business is famous and therefore a first-class service to the community. There is much in China's past to encourage the hope that such a development would be a natural and therefore a stable one, not liable to sudden disruption from internal causes. The main obstacles are the pressure of foreign capitalists and traders, coupled with the urgent need for capital in order to secure any industrial development, with lack of leadership, imaginative and practical, with time in which to work out experiments and let a difficult transition be peacefully accomplished. There is, I fear, also a lack of that degree of mutual confidence which is a prime condition of success.

Some experiments are being made that at least prepare the way for such a development. I found a few co-operative enterprises being developed in different centres. These are as yet small and little known, but if they succeed they cannot fail to have an effect out of proportion to their size. There are the model villages and towns, to two of which I referred, where education is being given to the workers and a degree of mutual confidence is being created which may make further developments possible. In speaking to Chinese employers I found them ready to listen to suggestions for improving conditions and for educating their employees even though I said quite plainly that such a policy would lead to a demand for a share in control which could not and ought not, in my opinion, to be resisted. Chinese are quick to see that a wide gulf between "capital" and "labour" will not be in the interests of the country, and there is in a number of employers a patriotic spirit which would prompt them to sacrifice some of their own profits if they could thereby work for the solidarity of the nation and a peaceful industrial development.

The Commercial Press in Shanghai is one of the finest examples of enlightened and progressive industrial enterprise under Chinese management. It is a noteworthy fact that the leading spirits are Christians and that the Press steadily refuses to put out any literature of an unhealthy character. The Press has a pay roll of over three thousand, the wages being relatively high and augmented by a bonus from time to time. Profit-sharing is practised, and many of the workers are also shareholders in the company. A pension system, savings bank, evening school, Y.M.C.A., dispensary and hospital are run by the firm. Mothers are given a month's leave of absence before and another month after child birth and two special bonuses of $5 each in connection with the event. In this business we have an illustration of what can be done already even under the present industrial system. Humane and wise management of a factory must contribute towards the right solution of this problem and the temper in which it is to be sought.

THE INDUSTRIALIZATION OF CHINA

Japan's industrial development has somewhat alarmed the Chinese, not merely because of the effect upon her policy in China and the Far East, but as an example of the way in which the industrial system may fasten on the body politic and even on the soul of a people. During the year 1921 there were over five hundred strikes in Japan. The great industrial centres were full of unrest. I was told by the leader of the Labour Movement that it was the Christian idea of the value of personality, entirely new, he said, to Japan, which was causing this unrest. I found Japanese employers alarmed, and eager in not a few cases to do what they could to improve conditions. The situation is tense and difficult and the Government recognizes the big problem of its increasing towns and industrial population.

China is entering upon the same path. Will it lead her into the same difficulties that Japan is facing and so strengthen the tendency towards the twin evils of materialism and militarism? Will it lead her along what the economic determinist would regard as the only road to emancipation—class-consciousness and class-war? Or is it possible that Chinese good sense, adaptability, patience, and peaceableness will enable this great nation to strike out a new line, to reach a basis for development that shall escape the most serious evils of modern industrialism? The answer to this question hangs in the balance. Its issue will be of immense significance, not for China alone, but for all the members in the family of nations. We Western peoples who have forced on her these perplexing problems owe to her what service we can render in helping her to solve them. Here is a missionary task of the first magnitude to be shared in by any who have the knowledge, sympathy and tact required, and who will be content to serve where they are asked, and will not seek to impose their views upon those they want to help. We owe it to China to give our best thought and some of our best people to her to help in the solution of a problem we have done so much to create.

CHAPTER X

THE NEW THOUGHT MOVEMENT.

In these pages we have necessarily concerned ourselves mainly with external movements. We now come back to a consideration of the problem of the inner life of thought and spirit. At the outset we glanced at the picture of ancient China, with her art, her literature, her philosophy, and her religious aspirations. We have seen something of the many influences, religious, commercial, political, that have had a share in making out of that ancient nation the China of to-day. Before we speculate about the China of to-morrow we shall try to understand how the thought life of China is responding to these external influences. Far more important and significant than the industrial and political changes in China is the change in her mental and spiritual life. This is much more difficult to study and estimate. Yet we cannot shirk the task. The whole object of this volume will be missed unless we can gain some true idea of what is happening in this sphere.

The changes in thought are both the result and the cause of many of the things we have already discussed. The impact of the West has quickened new thought, and new thought has led to re-adjustment in social and political life. It is therefore difficult to know just where to begin.

Perhaps it will be best first to deal with a movement which had no connection with European or American influence : I refer to the literary revival of the Ch'ing (Manchu) dynasty. During this period there were many scholars who, under a Chinese ruler, would, in all probability, have been engaged in government service, but who devoted themselves instead to a re-examination of the classical writings. They were not concerned with original philosophy, but they formed a school of patient textual critics, and they challenged the work of the commentators of the Sung and Ming dynasties. Around the writings of the sages a vast mass of commentary and interpretation has grown up in the course of the centuries, and this has created an orthodoxy which has amounted to an enslavement of thought. This tendency came to a head during the Sung dynasty, when an edition of the classics was published by imperial authority about the beginning of the eleventh century, with the title *The Correct Meaning*, and still more in the writings of Chu Hsi, who (about a hundred years later) composed in beautiful style those famous commentaries, whose influence on the literature of China " has been almost despotic."[1]

Not until the Ch'ing dynasty did any school arise which seriously challenged these " correct meanings." The patient work of Maon Se-ho (who published over 300 books on the classics) and other scholars did much to break the intellectual fetters with which Chinese students had been bound ; and in many respects they may be compared to our own textual critics, preparing the way for the later work of higher criticism. They reconstructed the texts of lost authors and delved into the rich mines of classical literature which awaited patient scholarly investigation. Although their work was little known there can be no doubt that it has been one of the chief preparations for the New Thought Movement. It is very important to recognize that we have here a purely indigenous effort of a very high order inspired

[1] Legge, *Confucian Analects*, p. 20.

THE NEW THOUGHT MOVEMENT

by a desire for truth and a scientific earnestness not less than that which has marked the advance of the West in invention and investigation of nature. It was essentially a revolt against mere tradition, in the conviction that truth must be faced whatever the consequences.

The second cause, without which this first movement could scarcely have led to any revolutionary changes, was the impact of Western thought. This came, in the first place, very largely through missionary schools and colleges and through the books written and translated by missionaries. For many years education along Western lines was resisted by China as a whole. To the Christian missionaries belongs the honour of persisting in the work of enlightenment against great opposition and misrepresentation. Now that Young China is turning eagerly to the West and is inclined to make light of this contribution and of the actual educational work of missions, it is not unfitting to stress this point. A leading non-Christian Chinese, on being asked when the revolution in China began, replied, "When Robert Morrison entered China," thus indicating his sense of the acknowledgment due to the foreign missionary as the initiator of progressive movements. This widespread work has not been confined to the comparatively small number who could enter the missionary schools and colleges. Through personal contacts, through magazines and, in particular, through certain books which had an immense circulation during the latter half of last century, the ideas behind Western civilization have been spread broadcast. Probably no book on Western life was at one time more widely read in China than Dr. Timothy Richard's adaptation of Mackenzie's *Wonderful Century*. It gave a graphic picture of what modern science had done for the West. Dr. Richard's name became a household word in every part of the Empire, and is to-day a name to conjure with, largely because in this book and other ways he sought to give China the very best and the very latest, in order that she might use these gifts for her own good.

Another avenue through which Western ideas came flooding into China was the influence of Chinese educated abroad. Beginning with the group of students sent to America in the early seventies of last century (of whom Tang Shao Yi is probably the best known) there has been a constant and generally growing stream sent both by the Government and the missions, and now increasingly going at their own charges. At the present moment it is largely these men and women who are leading the thought of China. Many are brilliant and well informed, and they are not simply imitators of the West. The real significance of the present position is that there is a considerable body of such Chinese who are keenly alive to Western ideas, ready to recognize how much China has to learn, but fully determined to save China from becoming a mere copyist. They are, in many cases, living in Chinese homes, much as their ancestors did, wearing Chinese dress and observing Chinese social customs, even though they have spent years living in Western style and dressed in American or British broadcloth. They have sat in classes with Western students and have shown their mettle time and again as able to hold their own in classes conducted in a foreign tongue and along unfamiliar lines. There are men among them who, even with these handicaps, have come out first in their classes. I wonder where an English young man of twenty would stand if he had to compete in a university class in a tongue other than his own with Chinese students, even if he had had several years in which to learn it before entering!

THE NEW THOUGHT MOVEMENT

There is no need to recapitulate the various external reactions due to the meeting of Western ideas and Eastern prejudices and principles as seen in the reforms of the young Emperor, the Boxer uprising, the later edicts of the Empress-Dowager, the birth of the Republic, and so forth. What we want to do is to see what methods and ideas characterize the so-called New Thought Movement and what is its deeper significance. The persistent aggression of Western nations, and the subtle infiltration of new ideas have combined to break up the rock which to Francis Xavier seemed as if it never would open. The pride of ancient China has given place to a new humility. The obstructiveness of the old scholar is replaced by the receptiveness of the new. The China into which new ideas were being pumped, as it were, against her will, is giving place to the China which is actively assimilating food; and the difference suggested by the two similes is a real one; the new China is discriminating, she is an active partner in the process, which is a life-process and not a mechanical one.

The New Thought Movement is only the latest manifestation of the way in which the life of China is shaped by her scholars. No student of China can be blind to the great influence exerted by the scholars upon her social and political development. We have already looked at some of the occasions when political events could only be explained in the light of the prevailing philosophy. The makers of Chinese history have been her thinkers far more than her generals. The sources of their power seem to me to have been two-fold. In the first place Chinese have an immense, perhaps even an exaggerated, respect for learning. Philosophy in China has been a practical thing. The maxims of the sages largely concern the ever-present problem of how men may live together in concord. That is to say, the classics are largely concerned with political philosophy, although, of course, abstract discussions had an interest for some of the great teachers. Thus the respect for learning is in part a conviction that learning is relevant to politics ; the wise man is the man with statesmanship, foresight, understanding of how men ought to act and of how they will act in association with one another. In the West the idea of learning has been at times largely divorced from that of practical statesmanship. The typical scholar is one who is withdrawn from life and in his own little world makes his contribution to abstract thought or to scientific theory. There is often an antithesis between the professor and the man of affairs. Broadly speaking, one may say that this antithesis is quite foreign to the thought of China. What is learning for if not to help men to live together peaceably ? In Confucius you have the combination of the sage and the statesman. He would not be reverenced in the one capacity had he not sought to apply his wisdom in the other. This conviction has expressed itself in the civil service examinations whereby the door to public service was opened only to the man of learning who had sat at the feet of the sages. Hence, when the scholars speak, the average Chinese believes that he is listening to words of exceptional political wisdom. I am not discussing the problem as to whether this is a good thing or a bad one and how far Chinese history shows the wisdom of entrusting political affairs to men of academic distinction. I simply state the fact as one of the reasons why the scholars of China have exercised, and are to-day exercising, so large an influence on her politics.

The second reason is, I believe, that through

her students China has for many centuries been much more of a democracy than appears on the surface. Every family in the Empire might have a member in the student body. The great ambition of the family would centre in the brilliant son who might, in course of time, through many painful experiences in the great examination halls, become one of China's " governing class." The very use of that phrase is an anomaly which illustrates the point. There has not been, in our sense, an upper or a middle class who have monopolized to a large extent the government offices. In the sense that the rulers of China might be drawn from any family, one may say that the local, and even the central government, has been democratic, a government by the people. The son who succeeded represented his family interests ; he came out of a community where he was known and whose life he knew ; his brother would be following the plough or sitting at the loom. Thus the official is in some degree in touch with the common life of the people, and the large student body from whom the officials were selected were a sort of informal democracy watching the government on the one hand and ever hoping to be able to play their part in it, yet on the other hand in touch with the life of the masses. Many would come from country districts even though their life was lived in the town, and in their correspondence with the home folks would give not only news from the city, but the latest ideas of the student body.

These considerations may help us to appreciate why it is that the student body has had, and still has, so much larger an influence in the development of the country than is, I suppose, the case in any other land. There is still little real democracy in China. The mass of the people are not educated enough to take an intelligent part in public affairs. Movements of reform have been limited to a small minority. But that minority is in a very strong position relative to the rest of the population. The most effective organ of democratic expression is the student body in association with the educational associations throughout China. It is this body which is the trustee of the past and the interpreter of the new thought which is seething in China to-day. It is this body, more than the military chieftains, with whom the future really lies.

The methods used by the leaders of the movement are of special interest. The printing press has, of course, been known in China for many centuries, and the traditional respect of Chinese for the written word gives great advantage to this means for propagating ideas. Young China has used the Press, with the modern improvements and the advantages which come from a first-class postal system, to an extent never before dreamed of in the country. It is no exaggeration to say that China has been flooded with magazines and papers during the last few years. At one time there were not less than four hundred magazines being published in the interests of the movement. They dealt largely with fundamental principles and with their application to every department of life. Books have usually been published in series, each part being of the nature of a magazine or pamphlet. Very many of these have been translations of foreign works. It is true that the number of magazines is now greatly reduced, but there are still about one hundred being published, which shows a large amount of literary activity among the students. In not a few cases students have themselves hawked the volumes or set up book stores where they could be obtained. In fact, we may say there has been a national tractarian move-

THE NEW THOUGHT MOVEMENT 205

ment not in the interests of authority, but in the cause of freedom.

Another interesting method has been the public lecture. Here again the movement uses and improves on an old Chinese custom. The scholar or storyteller may be found with his little group of listeners at many a tea-house and street-corner in every part of China. The modern lecturer may not so often go out into the open, although that is done, and I myself took part in an open-air meeting in Chengtu planned by the educational association in one of the large parks. Foreigners have been brought over to China in order to give Chinese students first-hand acquaintance with leaders of progressive thought in other countries, and the lectures given in various centres have been published far and wide. This method may only emphasize one aspect of the movement, but it is an important means of breaking down prejudice, as the foreigner comes, not on his own initiative, but as the guest of the Chinese themselves.

Another important method is the group discussion carried on in numbers of small societies all over the country. I came into touch with some of these and found that they were not only discussing problems in an abstract way, but also making social and educational experiments in order to express themselves and to try out their ideas. The sense of dissatisfaction with the present order is brought to a head in such groups, and at the same time there is, in some cases certainly, a serious purpose to study the best available literature, whether it be on a social, a scientific, an economic or a religious problem.

Far and away the most significant thing in the realm of method is the change which has been made in the written language. Here the reformers were dealing with one of the most deeply rooted traditions in China. The language of scholarship for all recorded history has been the *Wenli*, or classical language. This is a method of writing which depends for its effectiveness upon great condensation and upon a wealth of literary allusion which is utterly beyond the uninitiated. It has been the treasure of the élite only to be won after years of painful study, an insurance against superficial learning and a means of preserving continuity with the distant past. Generation after generation have laboriously acquired a language which probably never was a spoken one, and as each generation of scholars acquired it, they became the guardians of the heritage for their favoured successors. The examination system depended entirely on accurate scholarship of this type, and an essay written in the speech of the people would no more be looked at than an English composition would be considered in a Greek prose test.

Against this time-honoured language the leaders of the New Thought have tilted with all the enthusiasm of revolutionaries. The motive has not been destruction of the ancient classics, but rather the determination to open the storehouse to the general public. It has also been necessary to fashion a mobile language which could be readily adapted to express new ideas and to take in new phrases. The missionaries should have the credit of being the pioneers in this reform because they saw that the Bible of the people must be put into the language of the people. In spite of the fact that only light literature such as fiction was ever published in the ordinary vernacular, the Bible was so translated. The missionaries did for Chinese what Wycliffe did for English; they made the spoken language a fit vehicle for expressing the deepest truth. On this foundation the modern

THE NEW THOUGHT MOVEMENT

scholars have built as the Elizabethan writers followed Wycliffe. They have greatly enriched the language with new terminology; they have written their most scholarly works in the limpid, easy phrases of a living language instead of trying to crush these new thoughts into a dead one. The result is that they have opened to the common people the old learning and the new; they are well on the way to creating a reading China, in place of a little aristocracy of learning.

The *Bei Hwa*, or plain language, has won the day. The opposition was at first very bitter, as was only natural when a privileged class was threatened with the loss of its special privileges acquired through much painful effort. But the Government has now so far recognized the triumph of the new speech as to order the use of it for the text-books in all primary schools. It is an interesting fact that the final triumph in this sharp conflict came in connection with the decision of the Versailles Conference in the Shantung issue. The country was swept with a wave of popular feeling which demanded expression. The *Bei Hwa* was the weapon forged for just such an emergency. At once pamphlets and articles appeared all over China demanding a change in the Government and explaining the political situation. The new language was the only way of reaching the masses. The opposition was simply snowed under in the popular enthusiasm. What had been the hobby of the few became accepted as the national language or *Kuo Yü*. The pathway to knowledge had been blazed, so that the wayfaring man, though a fool, should not err therein.

This reform has not only made the treasures of learning available for the less educated Chinese; it has also made intercourse with foreigners much simpler. Very few who had not learned from childhood could hope to acquire a sufficient knowledge of the classics to appreciate all the allusions and to get the full flavour and meaning of what was written in *Wenli*. Modern Chinese thought, including the re-emphasis upon many aspects of the ancient philosophy, is now easily accessible to the foreigner who possesses an average knowledge of the language. The movement towards the unification of the spoken language has also received a great impetus, and even in places where a local dialect has been the only means of intercourse in the past many now learn to speak Mandarin. This is greatly facilitated by the phonetic script which is used to give the right pronunciation of new words for school children, and which, by its use for illiterates, is also tending to unify the spoken language. It will probably be many generations before the local dialects disappear or become so much modified as to differ, say, only as Yorkshire and Somersetshire dialects differ from one another. But we shall surely in time see the disappearance of the anomaly of a people with the same written language and with many quite different vernaculars. Whether the phonetic script will even take the place of the Chinese ideographs is a subject on which I do not venture to prophesy. On the one hand, there is sure to be a tendency in that direction in the interests of commercial efficiency, a more rapid education and better means of communication with foreigners. The learning of the ideographs takes an altogether disproportionate amount of the student's time, whether he be a Chinese child or a foreign adult. On the other hand, the character is so bound up with the history and inner nature of the people, is so rich a storehouse of thought and experience, and has such a strong hold on the affectionate regard of the nation that I do not look forward to its early disuse, nor could I do so with

THE NEW THOUGHT MOVEMENT 209

anything but deep regret. In these years of transition in particular I feel that China must hold to her own script. If it were given up, I fear it would be the first step towards the complete Westernization of China, a disaster of the first magnitude both for China and for the world. Happily there is no immediate prospect of anything like this taking place, but one cannot fail to see that there are strong reasons which might, under certain circumstances, bring such a movement into being. Perhaps the chief safeguard is the nature of the spoken language, which, being entirely monosyllabic, has very few distinct word-sounds. Where one sound has to do duty for many different meanings a phonetic script is liable to give the wrong meaning, a matter easily corrected in conversation, but of greater difficulty in communication by writing.

Enough has been said in regard to this revolution in language to show the driving power of the student movement. A literary tradition, thousands of years old, in a country proverbially conservative, has been overthrown in about five years. The credit belongs largely to the leaders in the National University, and in particular to Dr. Hu Shih (Suh Hu), a graduate of Cornell and Columbia, and a man of peculiar charm and personal force. His influence has spread throughout the country and he is far more the leader of China to-day than any general or politician. He and his friends are opening the treasure-house of ancient and modern learning to the man in the street, and are attempting to bring about that synthesis on the nature of which the future of China so largely depends. The struggle for the *Bei Hwa* has really been a struggle for the ideals of the New Thought Movement, and to these we must now give some attention.

To understand the New Thought Movement one

must contrast it with what was happening in China ten or fifteen years ago. At that time China was anxiously looking to the West in the belief that she needed Western ideas and inventions and methods in order to develop her resources, raise the standard of living and assume her place among the great Powers as Japan had done. Not least did she feel the need of an army and navy that would command respect and so enable her to resist foreign aggression. Self-interest and self-protection plainly indicated the need of going to school with the West. There was a determination to gain what she could of Western civilization mainly on its material side, and obviously to do this one must study in Western ways and, if possible, in Western schools.

Since then several things have happened. The Great War has given a shock to China and caused her thoughtful people gravely to question the value of Western civilization in certain of its outstanding results. A closer knowledge of Western lands by students and by coolies working in France, and through literature, has made many Chinese sceptical as to the advantages of our boasted civilization. To this must be added the moral revulsion caused by Japanese methods, in which China sees a too apt copying of European models. The failure of Versailles to remedy China's wrongs is another important factor in the growth of a new spirit.

While these influences have been causing many Chinese to question Western superiority, there has also been a deep conviction that all is not well with China herself. Her internal discords and weakness are patent to all. The much-vaunted democratic movement has not achieved inward peace and stability, and China's new rulers under the Republic have not, as a whole, shown any greater self-restraint in regard to peculation than did the old. In fact,

THE NEW THOUGHT MOVEMENT 211

many Chinese will tell you that the country as a whole has suffered rather than gained by the overthrow of the Manchu régime, bad as that had become. Those who are thinking about China's own condition and her place in the world are in a dilemma. To copy the West may mean a second Japan, only more so; to refuse to do so may mean weakness, decay and dissolution.

The group of young men who are guiding Chinese thought to-day are facing this dilemma by an effort on the one hand to discover the inner secrets of Western strength, and, on the other, to bring out the deepest meaning in their own philosophy, and so to effect a new synthesis on the intellectual and spiritual plane. They have set themselves the task not of copying the West here and the East there, but rather of creating a new thing through a deeper appreciation of all that is best in both. The task is supremely difficult, and for that reason it cannot be supposed that anything like complete success has yet been attained. Some will challenge this interpretation, because what they have chiefly seen in the movement seems to be wild excess and overstatement in one direction or another. They see manifestations which may be labelled as Bolshevism, free-love, atheism, ultra-nationalism, license and so forth. Such manifestations are inevitable in a time of intense mental and spiritual ferment. But they are not the most significant thing, and by a concentration on them one may miss the real significance of what is happening. No one can say whether the truer ideals of the movement will prevail or whether they will be lost in a welter of excess. But to assume the latter is to make that eventuality more probable, while to study and sympathize with what is best in the movement is at least to give this a chance of prevailing over the many dangers by which it is surrounded. Most of what I say is therefore a frank appreciation of the movement rather than an attempt to criticize it.

The leading ideas which are emphasized in the literature of the movement and by its leaders are not unlike those which characterize the movements of youth in other countries. Coming from Europe, where I had been able to make some study of the German Youth Movement and other similar manifestations, I was greatly struck by this similarity. This in itself is a symptom of the new age in which the progressive forward-looking thought of all nations tends to approximate. Is not this one of the most hopeful facts in a world where there is still so much discord and distrust ? Like the Youth Movement in Germany there is no central organization to whom one can appeal for an authoritative statement of what the movement stands for. Perhaps the chief uniting force is in the magazine known as *La Jeunesse* (Shing Tsin Nien), which was started in 1915 and has come to be recognized as giving expression to the aspirations and principles that are guiding Young China. But even this magazine has no authority beyond what it can gain by the intrinsic worth and acceptability of the ideas it publishes, and no doubt one of the chief reasons of its influence is just the fact that it does not assume to be an authority. It is characteristic of the movement to challenge all authority, to oppose organization as such, and to criticize strongly any attempt to impose ideas or fashions upon others. It represents a reaction against despotic government on the one hand and a rigid literary tradition on the other

This reaction seems to me to spring from a new view of the value of the individual and his rights in society. In the old patriarchal family the individual never had a chance of adequately expressing himself until he reached the position of *pater familias*, and when he got there his mind was already set and he tended to dominate all other members of the household. A man's life was ordered for him by rigid social requirements; marriage was arranged by the families often quite independently of the wishes of the parties most concerned and sometimes more in the interests of the family as a whole than in those of the bride and bridegroom; choice of occupation was very limited, choice of residence very rare. This system, with all its advantages for social coherence, tended to create the rebel type—and now that social ties are being weakened, the rebel is getting his chance. The New Thought Movement is psychologically in part a rebel movement. But it is more than this, and unless it be more than this it cannot be of the greatest lasting value. There is a new discovery of the meaning and possibility of human life, and this, I think, has mainly come through Christian channels, though not always so recognized. I used to wonder whether missionary education in China was not going too far in its emphasis on this truth or, at any rate, failing to emphasize the other aspect of life, that of social solidarity. There may have been some failure here, but the results show how ready China was to discover the meaning of personality, than which scarcely any greater gift could be given her from the West; for the worth of the person is in reality an assertion of the divine purpose and the possibilities of human life. The emphasis on personal worth is not permanently possible apart from belief in a personal God, and it is here that Chinese thought has, in my view, been most deficient.

How can this new wine be poured into the old bottles of Chinese social life without disastrous results? This is the great problem which I see, and it is here that the New Thought Movement should greatly help. In probing into the deeper meaning of Chinese philosophy it becomes apparent that the ruling ideas are related to the ever-present problem of social adjustment. It is true that the Confucian classics have much to say about the Chüin Tsï or Princely Man. His character and habits of mind are dwelt upon, and we are told that he must have sincerity, patience, earnestness, and so forth. But these qualities are needed in order that he may serve the community. His character is judged by social standards.

"The officer," we are told, "having discharged all his duties, should devote his leisure to learning. The student, having completed his learning, should apply himself to be an officer" (Analects Bk. XIX, Ch. XIII). And, again, "The scholar, trained for public duty, seeing threatening danger, is prepared to sacrifice his life. When the opportunity of gain is presented to him, he thinks of righteousness" (*Ibid.*, Bk. XIX, Ch. I).

If the Western emphasis on personality is not to act as a solvent on much that is admirable in Chinese life, it will be necessary to preserve a very strong sense of social duty. Whatever we may have to say about official corruption in China, and unfortunately there is much to be said about it, the highest thought of China has clearly seen that no community could persist without the belief in our all being members one of another. It is not by military prowess and individual self-assertion that the sages believed in creating harmony and good government. When Mencius was asked, "How can the kingdom be settled?" he replied, "It will be settled by being united under one." "Who can so unite it?" said the king. "He who has no pleasure in killing men can so unite it." "Who can give it him?"

THE NEW THOUGHT MOVEMENT

he was asked. "All under heaven will give it him," was the reply (Mencius, Bk. I, Ch. VI).

Young China to-day, in turning back to her sages, is following the path of wisdom. We in the West are beginning to see that pure individualism, the policy of *laissez faire* and unchecked individual enterprise, is disastrous. Can China avoid passing through such a phase ? There are many signs that the rebel spirit is intolerant of any form of constraint whether by government or social custom. Everything depends on whether Young China, bursting the bonds of outward restraint, is going to show a self-restraint, a poise, an inward discipline similar to that of her greatest leaders in the past.

Coupled, then, with the new emphasis on personality expressing itself in democratic movements, in freedom from social tyrannies, in æsthetic self-expression, and so forth, we find an emphasis on social service and a belief in peace and goodwill as the gifts which China should be bringing to the world. New ideas are tested not by their relation to the past ; are they orthodox or not ? They are tested rather by their reasonableness and scientific accuracy on the one hand ; will they fit the facts ? and by their social utility and practicability on the other hand ; will they work ? This is the temper in which Young China is setting forth upon her new crusade. Old and new alike are submitted to these tests. Chinese customs and Western innovations alike come under review. Young China believes that with this touchstone she will be able to create out of the blending of new and old the civilization which expresses her inner nature and is adapted to carry her forward in the general stream of human progress.

The movement may also be considered as an effort to achieve the threefold aim of human endeavour, truth, goodness and beauty. In the search for truth

Young China applies the methods of the West as used in scientific and historical research. Superstition of every form is challenged. There is a certain ruthlessness in the youth of China, as in other lands, a fearlessness of consequences which is willing to see anything go in the interests of truth. The great danger in such a spirit is that things of value may be sacrificed in the interests not of truth itself, but of an imperfect conception of truth. It cannot be said that the New Thought Movement has wholly escaped this danger, but when one considers the terrific obstacles that have had to be overcome, it need cause no surprise that there have been some mistakes.

In the quest for goodness the emphasis has certainly been laid upon a social rather than upon a personal good. The movement is intensely patriotic, yet at the same time it looks upon the task of China as not simply self-assertion, but rather as self-development for the good of the whole human family. The ideals are international in a general sense, though as regards the aggression of Japan or other foreign Powers, there is very deep resentment. The concern of the leaders is not mainly, however, to effect political changes, but rather to educate the people, to improve social conditions, to tackle the problems raised by the industrialization of China, and so forth. The social conscience is being quickened and efforts have been made for depressed classes, rickshaw men, children in factories, and so forth. It cannot be said that any large results have yet been achieved, but even the fact that attention is being directed to such objects is a hopeful feature in the situation.

In the third place the movement emphasizes the need for a truer appreciation of art and literature. It is even showing a tendency to substitute æsthetics for religion and to assume that man's instincts of

THE NEW THOUGHT MOVEMENT

reverence and his spiritual longings can be satisfied in this realm. One of the writers in the movement has expressed the point in these words : " We realize that true religion and literature embrace the same spirit. Consequently, however attacked by science religion may be, it still occupies a firm and proper place in literature. This is not to praise religion or to offer any apologies for religions, because they are really one in their fundamental spirit. Even though all the churches were overthrown, there would still exist in literature the essence and feeling of religion." This impersonal idea of religion seems to me inadequate as a dynamic to enable Chinese students to realize their high aims. But it may be that some of the religious teachers from the West have failed to appreciate the need for artistic expression of our deepest aspirations and ideals, and that the emphasis of the movement on this aspect of life is needed more than some Westerners think. Doubtless a place must be found in the higher life of China for the expression of that passion for beauty and those exalted ideas of art to which reference was made in the second chapter.

While the movement is not primarily political, it will have been clear that it is intimately bound up with the political development of China. Freedom in the realm of thought must express itself in free democratic institutions. There is almost an obsession on this point among the students. News has just reached me of a big inland city where three of the chief Government colleges are at a standstill because the students would not accept the principal appointed by the authorities and have elected their own. When I was in Peking, I had the unique experience of giving a sample lecture to the Government Higher Normal College, after which the students voted by show of hands in my presence on the question as to whether they would have the rest of the course. These are but trivial illustrations of a very urgent demand on the part of Young China to be mistress in her own house. One might say they are the effect upon the students of the sense that China is a mere plaything of the great Powers, the commercial magnates and her own military chiefs. They are saying in the only department of action open to them, "We will not have these men to reign over us."

The effect upon the women of China is perhaps even greater than that upon the men. There we have a problem of the first magnitude. Every progressive person must desire the emancipation of China's womanhood from the bondage of the past. But how can this be accomplished without loss too terrible to contemplate? The most remarkable change in China during the last ten or twelve years is the change in the status of womanhood. Women are going about freely; many are receiving a good education; they are demanding freedom from home restraints, a voice in the all important matter of marriage, and so forth. At a recent women's student conference my wife was to lead one of half a dozen sectional gatherings, her subject being "Freedom in the Home." All the other sections were depleted, and the whole conference gathered to hear her and discuss this burning topic. The New Thought Movement recognizes the equality of the sexes. It has not yet worked out its principles on this question, but it is standing for the Western idea of the home in which the newly-married couple shall be free to live their own life. Thus is challenged the very foundation of the ancient social structure of China.

Every student of contemporary history will realize the family likeness between this New Thought Movement in China and similar movements in other countries. That which gives the individual character

THE NEW THOUGHT MOVEMENT 219

to this movement is its relation to China's philosophical background on the one hand, and the suddenness with which she has been plunged into this new world of thought on the other hand. It is early to judge of the movement, and one has no right to assume that its present characteristics will be maintained. But I do not think it is altogether fantastic to compare it to the Renaissance in Europe. My friend Dr. Phillippe de Vargas, of Peking, has worked out this comparison in a paper read before the Wên Yu Hui (Literary Culture Society) in that city. He has noted the four factors of the Renaissance as being:—

1st. The STUFF of which the new civilization was made, i.e. the native mental and moral vigour of the Keltic-Teutonic peoples arrived at their bloom.

2nd. The PRECEPTOR of barbaric Europe's youth, i.e. the Hebraic-Hellenic teaching given mainly by the Church, with emphasis on moral and religious lines.

3rd. The DETERMINER OF THE CONSCIOUSNESS of the New Europe, i.e. the attacks of Oriental peoples.

4th. The STARTER of the new civilization, i.e. the impact of the Hebraic-Hellenic culture in its rediscovered freshness and glory.

To these four elements he compares the following similar elements in the Chinese Renaissance:—

1. The stuff of the new civilization—the Chinese people.
2. The preceptor—the scholarship of the Ch'ing period.
3. The determiner of consciousness—the aggressive West.
4. The starter—modern Western civilization.

This comparison is one of peculiar interest and suggests certain reflections with which we may close this chapter.

1. Comparing in each case the stuff of the new civilization, as he calls it, I am not disposed to rank the Chinese as one whit less capable mentally than the races of Northern Europe. We have a different development determined largely by the fact that the Chinese have chosen the life of agriculture, trade and learning rather than the life of warfare and wandering. The pause in the development of China is accounted for mainly by her extreme reverence for the past, her written language, which imposes so great a burden on the memory and gives little chance to the student to develop initiative and imagination, her crowded population, and the fact that her scholars did not use the inductive method and so never really started on the path that has led the West to such rich new fields during the last three centuries. To-day China's period of arrested development has come to an end and the mental enlargement and emancipation which are coming open up unspeakable possibilities. Whether Chinese will show skill in research and the plodding perseverance which have done so much to unlock new doors to Western scholars it is difficult to estimate. But I believe they will, and that China's contribution to scientific advance in the next century or two will be a very large one.

2. When we compare the second element, the preceptor, I am bound to confess that I do not think the Chinese classics with all their rich stores contain as much for human progress and betterment as did the Hebraic-Hellenic culture. But we cannot consider this element apart from the fourth, the starter, and here we have in the one case the rediscovery of the principles and ideas out of which the existing order had actually been shaped, and in the other case the impact of an entirely new set of ideas. That is to say, in the one case we have a readjustment of

THE NEW THOUGHT MOVEMENT 221

a civilization to its own origins, in the other case we have the reaction of two different streams upon one another. This leads me to the view that China's Renaissance may have even more momentous consequences for humanity than that of the fifteenth century in Europe. This is making a very great claim. Yet I think anyone who has been brought up in the Hebraic-Hellenic tradition, and who has entered deeply into the spirit of China, must feel that there are bewildering and alluring possibilities for the human race in the impact of these two streams of thought. The pity of it is that the serious attempt to meet this situation is almost confined to the Far East, and that Europe, which needs the same reinforcement, is not adequately sharing in the tasks of thought.

3. The problem in the mind of many will be the question as to what is to be the influence of all this upon Christianity in the Far East. Most of the leaders of the movement have expressed themselves as opposed to Christianity, and indeed to any religion in the fullest sense of that term. They regard Christianity as one of the outworn superstitions which must be discarded by thinking people. Mr. Ch'ien Yuan Tung, one of the recognized leaders of the movement, has recently expressed himself as accepting the historical Jesus as a great teacher whose views have been expounded by Tolstoi. He says that this writer has in his drama and novels exhausted the fundamental ideas of the Christian religion and left nothing unturned that ought to be turned to light. He believes that there are ideas in the New Testament which must be discarded in the light of modern knowledge and changed social conditions, and that the Old Testament is not important from the Chinese point of view. While admitting that Jesus Christ lived out His own

principles of universal love, he does not think that His followers have truly caught His spirit. He says: "We can do reverence to Christ, because He it was that had the revolutionary spirit and the courage that broke down old habits, created new conceptions, and slavishly imitated nobody. Instead of catching this great revolutionary spirit, Christians have merely worshipped Him, and have thus wronged Christ!"[1]

This may be said to represent the middle position. On the one side there are those who have formed the anti-Christian or anti-Religious Society and who follow the teachings of Bertrand Russell, and other Westerners, in identifying Christianity with all the wrongs done in the name of Christ by His weak and misguided followers. On the other side, there are some strong Christians who are recognized as true leaders of the movement and who are presenting their faith in a way that appeals to the scientific mind.

I think it may fairly be said that the New Thought Movement opens a new door for the presentation of the deepest aspect of the Christian faith. Challenging all authority, it is not going to be convinced by a purely authoritarian presentation, whether the authority be Church or Bible. But, broadly speaking, the mind of Young China is ready to consider truth presented in a clear way as something that will appeal to the inward sense of truth in the individual. While there is an element of sheer iconoclasm, impatient of any system that involves any kind of restraint, and while there is also an element of ultra-nationalism that despises Christianity as a foreign religion, there are many who sincerely desire to find an answer to China's need and are willing to listen to truth from whatever quarter it may come. To this more earnest and reverent mind the Christian faith will appeal

[1] *Chinese Recorder*, October 1922.

THE NEW THOUGHT MOVEMENT

just so far as it is seen to have social value and to face fearlessly all the facts of science and history.

In his treatment of reform movements in India, J. N. Farquhar shows how even those who oppose Christianity are actually applying the standards of Christ to judge the theory and practice of rival systems. Something of the same kind is happening in China. In spite of much failure in vision and in action on the part of His followers, Jesus Christ is increasingly seen by the youth of China as One who commands their respect and fulfils their ideal of a human life. If the efforts of Christian teachers is merely to impose on Young China a foreign type of thought and life with little or no reference to China's past, the great body of young Chinese will turn away from it, and quite rightly. If it be rather to lead them to see how their own deepest aspirations can be fulfilled, to work out to a higher point all that is true in China's social life and philosophy, to give fresh courage and hope in the task of creating a new China, in short, to help China to be worthy of her own past and a helpful member of the family of nations, then the Christian message will be welcomed by all the best elements in the New Thought Movement.

The National Christian Council for China has been formed during the past year, largely under the leadership of the younger generation of Chinese Christians, in the hope that the Christians of China can stand together as one man, for the adequate presentation of the Christian faith to the mind and heart of China. Very much depends on how this task is tackled. It is my own conviction that there is in the Christian faith, in its simple essence, something which China needs to bring to perfection this amazing movement of youth. If a spirit of arrogant self-sufficiency should creep into it, if its leaders shut out light that comes from suspected sources or through imperfect channels, if its ideals of truth and beauty and personal freedom are not grounded in the belief that the universe is ordered by One who is a free person Himself, the embodiment of all truth and beauty, then I fear a collapse, a failure to carry through to any great accomplishment the splendid dreams of this new era. But if China's young manhood and womanhood see in Christ the answer to the riddle of the universe and the crown of China's own life, I believe this movement will give to the world a gift beyond words to express.

CHAPTER XI

CHINA'S GIFT TO THE WORLD.

We now come to what is by far the hardest part of our task. We must forsake the historical method and attempt to look into the future. While I entirely disclaim any power to forecast China's destiny or her influence upon the rest of the world, I think we may look at the present direction of movement, estimate the strength of the various forces and see what possibilities open up before us as we engage upon this task. We may also make certain suggestions as to what is needed on the part of China herself and on the part of other nations if the better possibilities are to be realized and the worse avoided.

Three broadly-differentiated possibilities open up before China to-day. The question as to which of them will be followed depends partly upon China and partly upon the nations with which she has to deal. For good or ill China's fate is now bound up with that of the whole family of nations. There may be some who would like to see it otherwise, and who wish that China might still pursue her age-long course in solitary glory. I sometimes meet those who say, for example, of foreign missions to China, "Why not leave China alone? She has not asked for our civilization or our commerce or our religion. She would be better without them. We have no right to force them upon her." Such talk is, at this stage of history, entirely beside the mark. A hundred years ago there might have been wisdom in it; at any rate, we might have discussed the issue with some hope that the decision reached in debate could be translated into politics. To-day, the discussion is purely academic, and we need not enter upon it. I only mention the matter to insist upon the point that our interest lies in an entirely different direction. We are concerned to see that the contacts which we recognize to be inevitable shall be of the right kind and made in the right way. Our task is not to dam the stream but to direct its force into the most productive channels.

Now, it is a curious and somewhat alarming fact that Western influences are very much greater in China than the West itself at all appreciates. What is happening in the main is not that a deliberate and thought-out policy is directing the action of Western nations in their relations with China, but that at a hundred unobserved points this influence is being exerted, and that most people in England and other Western countries neither know nor care about what is happening. Many things are being done in our name, or in such a way as to involve that name, about which most of us are sublimely ignorant. The West is judged not by the abstraction which we call Western culture, but by the acts of this merchant, that missionary or the other consul, and by just those books and papers which happen to reach the people of China. Without any doubt, the biggest fact in China to-day, that which is most creative of difficulty and most seriously affecting the whole nation, is the impact of the Western world. And yet we of the West are almost unaware of the fact that we are thus disturbing the life of this great nation. We are engrossed in our own problems and very rarely think of China at all.

Arnold Toynbee, in his recent treatment of the

CHINA'S GIFT TO THE WORLD 227

Near and Middle East, has observed the same point, and the student of the Far East cannot fail to be struck by the interesting similarities as well as the curious differences in the two problems. At the beginning of his volume, *The Western Question in Greece and Turkey*, he pictures the savage watching an eclipse of the moon and unable to realize that it is being blotted out by nothing less than the shadow of the earth on which he stands. So the shadow of the West is cast on the East, and we stand by scarcely able to realize the true cause of the trouble. Mr. Toynbee says : " Just because we are aware of what passes in our own minds, and know that interest in Eastern affairs is almost entirely absent from them, it is difficult for us to realize the profound influence on the East which we actually, though unconsciously, exercise. This conjunction of great effect on other people's lives with little interest in or intention with regard to them, though it is common enough in human life, is also one of the principal causes of human misfortunes. . . . Either the overshadowing figure must turn its head, perceive the harm that unintentionally it has been doing and move out of the light ; or its victims, after vain attempts to arouse its attention and request it to change its posture, must stagger to their feet and stab it in the back." [1]

This passage suggests the problem which confronts China. The three possibilities to which I referred may be described as disintegration, denationalization and reintegration. The first of these seemed imminent twenty-five years ago. At that time China, under an effete monarchy, beset by foreign Powers, self-seeking and jealous of one another with little appreciation of or reverence for the country they were threatening, seemed on the point of collapse economically

[1] Op. cit., p. 2.

and politically. The policy of spheres of influence seemed likely to lead on to open partition; one looked in vain for any force strong enough to hold back the forces either of inward decay or of external pressure. As we have seen, two things happened. Internally China began to awake and through her students and commercial men showed a power of thought and action which surprised those who judged her only by her inefficient and corrupt statesmen. The change from without was inaugurated by America and backed by Great Britain, when the policy of the open door was announced and followed up by that of the International Consortium. This held up, for a while at any rate, the aggressive policies of Western States. China has been given a breathing space, but it cannot be said that the danger of disintegration is wholly passed. Something more is needed in both directions, and in particular China must awaken yet more fully to the activities of the situation and set her own house in order.

The second possibility is that China may to a large extent lose her distinctive character in her efforts to meet the West on its own terms. It cannot be said that Japan has avoided this danger. She has certainly been successful in meeting Western aggression. She has learned her lesson very well. But in doing so it seems to me that Japan has lost something of real value, and may lose yet more. Her recent efforts in the sphere of economic imperialism may be more true to her inner nature than would similar action be in the case of China. But I fear that what Mr. Toynbee says of Turkey is in some measure true also of Japan. He says: "Though the Ottoman Empire, by adopting Western methods, has achieved what seemed impossible a century and a half ago and has survived until our day, it has never so far gone much beyond the minimum degree of Westernization necessary to save it, at any given moment, from going under. It has borrowed more technique than ideas, more military technique than administrative, more administrative than economic and educational."[1] The extreme forms of nationalism now seen in Japan are the product of the mixing of two civilizations, and the realization on the part of Japanese leaders that, while she needed to accept many Western ideas and methods in order to save herself from destruction, she had nevertheless something which she must preserve. How far she has succeeded it is too soon to say. Certainly her present state can only be regarded as a phase through which she must pass either to a more complete Westernization of her institutions or to a new and deeper synthesis of East and West.

In the case of China the problem is even graver. China's nature would be even more deeply violated were she to become a militarist and imperialist people, and the world would thus lose one of the chief remaining forces in the direction of sanity and peace. The events I have traced in this volume are tending to drive China into militarism and into other Western vices. It is amazing to me that the movement in this direction is not far stronger than it is. China has had every provocation, and yet, on the whole, has kept her head. Nevertheless the militarists of China have now an immense power, and it is hard to see how she is to come through the present phase and how the civil authority is actually going to assert itself over the military. The same kind of struggle is going on in the industrial world, and it is even more difficult to see how China is to achieve an industrial system that is not a mere copy of Western capitalism. The signs of the times seem to point to a somewhat long period during which China,

[1] Op. cit., p. 13.

in the struggle to avoid the first alternative, disintegration, falls a victim to the second evil and becomes so deeply influenced by the West as to lose, in some measure, her own soul. I suppose no one who knows China would anticipate so complete a submergence of her ancient culture as fell upon the civilization of Central America under the influence of the more virile and dominating European nations. But I can imagine a period when the practical necessities of the case will impose upon China an industrial and political development so foreign to her own genius as to cause quite a long submergence of some of the finer elements in her own culture. While we cannot draw any hope from the contemplation of political and commercial happenings, we can see in the world of thought and religion some indication that this disaster may be avoided.

The only other alternative, as I see it, is that new synthesis which I have spoken of as a re-integration. Only by boldly grasping the nettle will the sting be avoided. To copy the methods of the West in commerce, politics or religion, and to seek to preserve unchanged the ancient springs of conduct, is to court disaster. The mere use of methods may seem to be a small thing, but sooner or later the methods one uses dictate one's philosophy of life. A man cannot go on using a fraudulent system or practising brutality without warping his moral sense or brutalizing his finer instincts. A nation cannot devote itself to the perfecting of military methods without being enslaved by the spirit of militarism. There is no solution for China along these lines. If she simply copies Western models of method, she will inevitably become Westernized to her own great loss.

This is where we see the significance of the New Thought Movement. The attempt to search out the inner significance of Western institutions must be prosecuted with patience and sympathy. A critical judgment must be brought to bear upon all that the West has to offer. That which is good must be understood, assimilated and worked over by Chinese minds, and it must be brought into relation to all that is best in Chinese life and thought. Every great advance in history seems to have been in some measure a re-integration, the mixing of strains of thought on types of personality that have developed on somewhat different lines, and the production of a new thing. Stagnation is due to inbreeding, and if the process is carried too far, the impact of another strain may lead to utter decay, and the submergence of one type. We have seen how China's civilization preserved its peculiar character in spite of the impact of foreign cultures so that it might be said that China conquered her conquerors. These other civilizations, in the main, proved unable to break up or seriously affect the strong social and philosophical system on which China's life was based. Perhaps Buddhism had more effect than any other, but even Buddhism scarcely turned the main stream of Chinese thought, although greatly affecting the lives of her people in certain ways. Broadly speaking, Buddhism was more deeply affected by China than was China by Buddhism.

China suffered from two causes. In the first place her early development of a high type of civilization left her *facile princeps* among the surrounding peoples. She developed rapidly to a point far in advance of her time and had no serious rival to challenge her supremacy. In the second place she was geographically so situated that she lost the stimulation of interchange of thought with the civilizations developing around the Mediterranean basin. The occasional contacts were not sustained enough to lead to any real mutual understanding even in the time of Kublai Khan, when we see the nearest approach to a meeting of Europe and China. For one system of thought to remain in isolated possession of the field for upwards of two thousand years is a phenomenon for which we have no parallel in European history. This seems to be one of the chief causes for the lack of progressive development in China. No doubt there were others such as the nature of the written language with its enormous demand upon the memory, the large measure of contentment among the people generally, and so forth.[1]

Be that as it may, we have now the phenomenon of a civilization long holding undisputed sway over the minds of millions, meeting another civilization no less virile and much more aggressive. The problem centres round the nature of the resulting product. Has the process of inbreeding been carried so far as to involve the absorption of the old by the new ? Young China answers this question with an emphatic negative. The very fact that her own scholars are probing into the secrets of Western progress goes far to show that she is right in making this reply. No easy superficial adjustments will meeet the case. It is not by working for quick returns that we shall solve the problem of China to-day—whether we expect these in a rapidly democratized government, in a Westernized army, in a wholesale acceptance of a foreign religion, or in the develupment of a commercial system duplicating that of London or New York. The real revolution in China has scarcely begun. Foreign observers have been critical and cynical in regard to the results of what has been

[1] An interesting discussion of the problem will be found in Mr. Wells's *Outline of History* (pp. 312–16), and also in Hubbard's *The Fate of Empires*. To these I would refer the reader, as it lies somewhat outside the main purpose of this chapter to deal more fully with the matter.

so styled. This change was a mere incident in the big thing that is happening under the surface and has gained quite a false prominence in the thoughts of both Chinese and foreigners. The Chinese word for revolution, Ge Ming, is, I believe, derived from a passage in a very ancient volume, *The Book of Changes*, which may be rendered as follows :

"Nature changes and so the seasons fulfil their times. Tang and Wu [were those on whom came the] *Change of Plan* (Ge Ming). [The change came] in full accord with [the will of] God and in complete response to [the needs of] man. How great is the time of Change ! "

Here we seem to catch a glimpse of the inevitableness and the significance of revolutionary changes. With a certainty like that of the changing seasons, the affairs of men move on from one stage to the next. The real revolution has two aspects—the fulfilment of a divine purpose and the satisfaction of a human aspiration. The new synthesis is being worked out in some far greater way than any of us can see. The West brings its doctrine of individualism based upon a conviction that Heaven is no impersonal force or blind destiny, but a creative loving mind, one who can truly be called our Father. China brings her massive social philosophy, a system representing the last word of the East on the principles which should bind men together in a living bond of responsibility and service. From the deeper blending of these two strains of thought who can tell what may be born ? Mazzini's words come with peculiar significance to the student of this wondrously interesting problem : " Life is one ; the individual and society are its two necessary manifestations ; life considered singly and life in its relation to others. Flames kindled upon a common altar, they approach each other in rising, until they mingle together in

God." Is the gift of China to the world to be a new light upon this age-long problem, to show new directions in which human society can approximate to the ideal that is to the divine purpose, the end of all our living?

Turning from this speculation, let us enquire into some of the conditions that should help to save China from the dangers of the first and second causes and make it possible for her to follow the third. First, let us look at the matter from China's own point of view, considering what internal changes are indicated, and then let us try to find out what policy on the part of Western nations will be of the largest service to China in the near future. I cannot pretend to deal with these questions in the order of urgency, because several must be worked at concurrently and they touch widely different regions of life.[1]

1. *China needs a strong, unified, constitutional government.* I am by no means an ardent advocate of the modern State idea, and I think many evils of Western life can be directly traced to over-centralization and to a false theory of the State. Nevertheless I feel sure that if China is to maintain her own culture and to progress in the right direction she greatly needs a strong, united government. I do not believe this can be brought into existence save by some system of Federated Provinces, with a large amount of autonomy. It may even be necessary at this stage to grant more power to the Provincial Assembly than will be ultimately desirable, because there is so much natural distrust of any central government, and so much fear that any Parliament sitting in Peking, however elected, will become the tool of the militarists. The Southern and Western Provinces will not come in on any

[1] Compare also the closing sections of Chapter V for certain practical suggestions.

system which does not give them very considerable powers, and much could rightly be sacrificed at this stage to avoid further fighting. The most perplexing problem is how can China shake off the iron grip of her own militarists and re-establish the civil power as supreme. The military leaders command large sums of money, and can use their financial power to strengthen their hold on the machine of government. One after another has disappointed expectations by proving his promises of reform to be empty and by using his power for selfish ends. Such a degree of enlightenment among the troops as would make them unwilling to move without guarantees of constitutional reform is hardly to be expected in the near future. It is possible to imagine the lesser generals agreeing that unity and constitutional government must be established so as to bring the war-lords to reason. I cannot say that I expect an early establishment of the kind of government I desiderate, but I believe much could be done by agreement among the leading commercial men in the country. The economic argument seems to be the one most likely to convince the militarists, and if the banks and financiers of China could combine on a policy and in the support of a few strong personalities who could carry it out, I think it would not be long before a move was made in the right direction. It would be necessary that the commercial and educational forces should unite, for the latter have great power among the common people. The recent appointment of people's delegates to Washington by the combined Educational Associations and Chambers of Commerce all over the country shows that such a concordat is not impossible. I believe a well-thought-out policy, including financial reorganization, judicial reform, electoral legislation, and a definite plan for the disbandment of many of the troops and their absorption into civil life, a scheme of provincial self-government and a federal Parliament, would rally many of the best minds in China, and if supported by the bodies mentioned, by local guilds and individual leaders of probity and ability, would soon appear as an alternative policy which no militarist could afford to oppose. I cannot here go into details on the various matters and it would be somewhat presumptuous to do so. But I feel that a main difficulty is that there is no intelligible programme before the public which commands the assent of substantial persons. The militarist is condemned for self-seeking and domination by his personal force. The reformers of the school of Sun Yat Sen are condemned for a somewhat wild excess and a failure in constructive statesmanship. Those who hold a middle position are constantly turning to catch the support of one side or the other and lack the strength to take their own line and press forward with it in face of criticism. Meanwhile the common man suffers all the time. Brigands abound; commerce languishes; laws are not enforced; uncertainty prevails. The need for a unified national policy is patent to all observers.

From the point of view of Western nations, this need is almost equally great. It cannot be expected that foreign enterprise in China will go forward or that money will be lent to her for her development unless China shows that she can handle her own affairs with vigour and integrity. At present there is hesitation on the part of foreigners and foreign Governments, because they do not know which way the cat will jump. If China could reorganize her political system and present a united front to the world, there would soon be a larger disposition to help her, or, shall I say, a greater possibility for that disposition which already exists to express

CHINA'S GIFT TO THE WORLD 237

itself. China's friends in other lands are often perplexed and paralyzed by this inner weakness and disunion which they believe to be a temporary phase, largely due to Western influences, as we have seen, but which so long as it persists, stops the mouth of those who would advocate her cause.

2. *China needs a higher moral standard among her public men.* I have already referred to some leading Chinese citizens who are notable examples of the combination of intelligence and honesty. I should be the last to assert that such qualities are not to be found in China. But I cannot close my eyes to the fact that this lack of public honour in many of China's leading men is one of the gravest dangers threatening her successful emergence from her present perils. When the Republic was proclaimed many hoped that a new era had dawned and that peculation and graft would come to an end. These hopes have been sadly disappointed. Every business man in the Far East knows that in commercial dealings Chinese have a high standard of honesty, comparing favourably with that of any nation. Why is it, one wonders, that a similar standard is so uncommon among her officials ? When the public purse is in the keeping of Chinese, the temptation to take from it seems often to be uncontrollable. Again and again China has suffered from men of reputation and standing who have preferred personal profit to public good. How few are the Chinese of whom one could write what Livy wrote of a great Roman : " The following year died Publius Valerius, by common consent the foremost man in the arts of war and peace. His fame was immense ; his private property was so scanty that there was not enough to pay the expense of his funeral. He was buried at public cost." (Livy II, 16.) The creation of this type of public servant is an even more pressing need

than the establishment of a unified government or
the reorganization of the finances. The fact that
business morality is high, leads to the hope that
some of China's statesmen in the future may be
drawn from the realm of commerce. I also believe
that the Chinese Christian Church has a large contribution to make in this realm. But it is possible at
once to quicken public opinion so that the demand
that such men be sought and be given positions
of trust may make itself heard. It is also possible
to introduce into public life certain very necessary
safeguards which honest officials would welcome
and which would check the dishonest. Publicity of
all public accounts with full and accurate details
of expenditure, a reliable system of audit, plans for
the impeachment of unworthy officials, adequate
salaries and rules preventing public officials from
being financially interested in undertakings that
might be helped by their official acts—these are
among the more obvious safeguards which would
materially help in the direction indicated.

3. *China needs to work out her own industrial system.* Far more thought should be directed to this
question. I could not pretend to have reached any
conclusion in regard to it, but I am persuaded that
an unthinking acceptance of the competitive and
capitalistic system as evolved in the West will mean
disaster for China. I do not believe that State Socialism is at all possible at present, both because of the
low degree of general education and because of the
weakness of the Government. I doubt in any case
whether any highly centralized system is true to
Chinese ideas. We have already seen some of the
factors in the problem and I cannot do more here
than urge that Chinese financial and business leaders
should get together with her students of economics
and with sympathetic Western business men and

CHINA'S GIFT TO THE WORLD 239

economists and try to think out lines of progress. It is probable that many experiments will have to be made, and not a few of these may fail through lack of some of the essential conditions of success. A measure of paternal or patriarchal government may be needed for a generation or two. But much depends on whether this is animated by the desire for personal profit and power or by an idea of public service directed to a larger development of industrial self-government when the time is ripe. China might well give an example to the world of a country passing by peaceful stages from the stage of agriculture and home industries to that of large-scale production. The common-sense and adaptability of her people, led by those who can use the experience of other countries and wisely relate it to China's own system, might enable her to do what no other country has done. This would indeed be a gift to the world.

4. *China needs to improve her system of communications.* In one sense this is only a single item in a large programme of industrial development, and I am not so much concerned here to urge the accelerating of that process as to point out the importance of development in other directions not less rapidly than in this one. Nevertheless, I introduce this point because of its relation to other aspects of the question. To meet the varied economic problems which beset China to-day it is obvious that the building of roads and railways, and the reconstruction of canals and the opening up of harbours, are prime necessities. One of the great difficuties in the way of normal trade and in meeting special emergencies is lack of transport facilities. As already mentioned, I think this work should come increasingly under the central government, and herein is an additional reason for urging my first point. Over and above this there is the fact that improved communication will help

to unify the country, to open up remoter places to new ideas, to facilitate the movement towards a common spoken language. and to check lawlessness and brigandage. The Roman instinct was true in driving great main roads through a conquered country so as to make the new government effective. China's problem of unsettlement and disunion will not be fully solved without a considerable development of her means of internal communication.

5. *China needs greatly to strengthen her educational work.* No problem in China to-day deserves more attention than the increase and improvement of her education. The remarkable progress already made shows what can be done. A new educational system has been evolved in the space of some ten years. Schools, colleges, educational associations, a vast output of text-books, speak to the earnestness with which the country is facing her task. At times one is discouraged to find very inefficient work, the name of Western education without the thing, extremes due to a superficial acceptance of ideas that are not understood. But taking the country as a whole and considering all the difficulties faced, I am amazed that so much has been done. There is a vast deal more to do. Teachers are often trained in a very theoretical way and supplied with many more ideas than they can assimilate; there is far too much reliance upon text-books; skilled inspection is sorely needed; students are put through their examinations by authorities who are more concerned to save their face than to ensure good scholarship. I think one of the chief dangers is that great principles, such as freedom and democracy, have become too cheap. Everyone talks in such terms. Many have not grasped their meaning in any fundamental way. I am not greatly concerned for the rapid extension of schools

CHINA'S GIFT TO THE WORLD 241

in China. I am concerned that what is taught should be far more thorough, and that teachers should be trained to think for themselves and lead their students to do the same. A teacher who knows only his textbook is afraid of questions lest he should be floored. China needs teachers who will set their faces against mere memory work, in which their students excel, and force them to work their own way through their problems. The schools need to make a special study of how to present new ideas so that they may be related to old customs. For example, the problem of freedom in relation to the social system should be tackled boldly and constructively. Students should be helped to see that they must accept certain limitations and conditions in order to work out any true self-development. Patriotism must be related to the ideal of international service. Now that the ethical teachings of the sages are somewhat at a discount much more thought should be given to the building of character.[1]

6. *China needs to reorganize her judicial system.* One of the chief complaints that China makes in regard to Western Powers is the continuation of extra-territoriality. While some of us would be willing, as individuals, to forego these rights and trust ourselves to the Chinese authorities, it is not to be expected that any considerable number of foreigners would take a course attended now with so much risk. There is still far too much corruption in the Chinese courts to give any assurance of fair dealing, and the laws should be altered so as to make torture impossible and to reduce sentences generally. Penal history shows that the effect of lighter sentences is not, as some fear, to increase crime, and I have no doubt that the experience of other countries would be repeated by China. In

[1] See also reference to *Adult Education*, pp. 97–8.

Chinese courts the object is to secure satisfaction to the aggrieved party even more than to punish the guilty, and that is so far to the good. I do not think China should simply adopt British or other Western judicial and penal methods. But I think that a careful study of the best writings on these questions, a larger understanding of the causes of crime and a more persistent effort to remove them, along with an improvement of the courts and a better system of appeal, would lead to such advance and would not only greatly benefit China, but also create a new confidence in her on the part of Western Powers, leading before long to the surrender of extra-territorial rights and the need for treaty ports and concessions. China would thus have taken a big step towards becoming mistress in her own house.

I do not, of course, suppose that these points cover all that is to be said on the question of what China can do to meet her present difficulties. On financial reorganization I have scarcely touched. Great evils like gambling and opium-smoking, which urgently need attention, I have not even mentioned. But I think if the matters I have specified were to receive the attention they deserve, China would soon be well on the way to discovering how to deal with many other questions. She would be doing her part to fit herself for a worthy place in the family of nations.

What do the other members of the family owe to China ? Here one has to begin with the frankest recognition of their failure hitherto to act the part of brothers in any large and consistent way. Again and again they have appeared rather as thieves and robbers, and no one can blame China if she has been unwilling to enter such a family. Now that she is moving into the circle, should we not seriously consider how to mend our ways ? If the West is to gain from her contact with China those things which China undoubtedly has to give, it is high time that the West treated her in a different way.

1. *The West must give China time to work out her salvation.* Perhaps the deepest tragedy in this whole story has been the way in which slow-moving, patient China has been rushed off her feet by the impetuous West. A little more patience, a little more understanding of her difficulties, and can there be any doubt that China and the West would have met and found fellowship with far less friction and misunderstanding ? The breathless pace of Western life has been too much for China. The worker on the land meets the town labourer and listens with wonder to all his tales, unable to follow the quick changes of his thought. But the worker on the land may be thinking deeper thoughts, far more worthy to be perserved for the enrichment of our common life. So China, thinking her long thoughts, has met this impetuous, pushing stranger, and because she could not at once learn his jargon and follow his example, he has voted her a dullard and only fit to be bullied. The time has come when all this should cease. China may yet tax our patience as she has done in the past. We may be exasperated and anxious to quicken the pace. But if we understand the things that belong to our peace and to the peace of China, we shall be very careful not to lose our patience or our temper. China has had too much interference from foreign Powers, even sometimes quite well meant interference. Pushing in, even to help, may damage unintentionally. If China asks for help, that is another matter. Advice is perhaps justifiable—at least, I have acted on this principle in this chapter. But any attempt to rush China into this or that policy seems to me to be fraught with danger. In picking men for diplomatic service in China the first

quality demanded should be patience. My motto for the next ten or twenty years would be: "Let China have a chance to see what she can do for herself."

2. *The West must seek to understand China better.* It is well that the old idea of the Chinese as semi-civilized barbarians has largely disappeared. But it must not be replaced merely by a vague sense of China's greatness and ancient splendour. We need to know what are the sources of such greatness. We need to concentrate attention not on the queer, superficial differences between Celestials and ourselves, but rather on the deeper fact of our common humanity and on the real significance of those elements in Chinese life that at first sight baffle us. Such a study is its own reward. It brings insight into aspects of human life which we should otherwise overlook; it quickens our imagination; it helps us to join in this common quest for a new synthesis between two such different civilizations. For it is not only China that is in danger of loss through in-breeding and prejudice relative to other types of thought than her own. It may fairly be said that the students of China are far more alive to the fact that they have something to gain from the West than are the students of Europe and America to the converse. Yet both are true, and our loss from such blindness will not be small.

Such patient effort to understand China cannot fail to develop a deep respect. Intercourse between nations as between individuals can only be truly based if there is mutual respect. The old contempt must wholly disappear. Yet how slow it is to go! Why, we are even fostering it in our plays and our movies. The other day my youngest son told a school-fellow that three Chinese gentlemen were coming to stay at our home. He was warned against

CHINA'S GIFT TO THE WORLD

them on the ground that they were sure to kill him, and when he remonstrated and said they were good men and friends of his father, the boy (of about ten years of age) answered that he knew all about Chinamen; they were cruel, wicked people; he had seen lots of them at the pictures! The incident may seem to be laughable, but it is full of terrible warning. For every person who reads such a volume as the present one, there are hundreds of thousands who see the pictures. Children are growing up with this false idea of the Chinese and of other races, and these children will be the makers of public opinion, the virtual creators of national policies in years to come. The poison is a deadly one, and some antidote must be provided. These considerations should give one furiously to think.

3. *The West must show China that she will deal with her problems in an absolutely fair way.* The distrust of Western nations which followed the betrayal of Versailles has been one of the most serious facts in China's relations with the West. It gave China the conviction that even when her case was unanswerable and was presented at the bar of humanity, her voice would not be listened to, because she could not back it by cold steel. Such an impression was disastrous both for China and for the West. Unless it can be removed (and Washington has done something to remove it), one of the chief causes tending to turn China from her true path will remain. In the work of the League of Nations we of the West have another chance. The Opium Commission of the League is important, not merely because it is dealing with a very grave evil that threatens the life of China, but because, according to the sincerity and thoroughness with which the matter is tackled, the West has yet another chance of showing her honest goodwill. If real justice is done to China,

and if Western nations can turn from profit and deal fairly with her, they will be doing the finest thing they can to show China that they really mean to deal with her as a sister nation, and they will in truth and not in word only be welcoming her into the family.

4. *The West should give China the chance of seeing the best aspects of her civilization.* Often Western nations have presented to China mainly their less attractive side. The mailed fist or the gunboat, the unscrupulous trader pressing his opium on China, the traveller patronizing or supercilious—these are manifestations that we have cause to be heartily ashamed of. Happily the Chinese of to-day are shrewd enough to discriminate between the different aspects of our civilization and are willing to receive the good while they reject the bad. But it should be the earnest aim of all good Europeans and Americans to bring to China those things of which we have no cause to be ashamed. China has called to her aid advisers and lecturers and specialists from foreign lands ; she has welcomed the splendid service of foreign administrators like Sir Robert Hart, who have made China's good their chief interest ; she is not slow to recognize all that has come to her through the widespread work of Christian missions. In this last sphere I have already pointed out that an element of patronage and a desire merely to proselytize have to some extent marred a great service. But it is increasingly true that the missionary movement is inspired by the desire to bring to China what is indeed the best thing we have to offer and to give her the chance to receive it and adapt it to her special needs. Believing as I do that the teaching and spirit of Jesus Christ are the source of the finest living and thinking in the West, and that they have helped to save us from our natural tendencies to

harshness, pride and impatience, I consider that in offering these to China, the West is at least seeking to make some honourable amends for the display of harshness, pride and impatience in many of our dealings with her. If the work of missions can display the opposite qualities—kindliness, humility and patience—there is no doubt that it will do something to soften the contacts and to purge away our sins. But it can do more than this. There is an ever new quality in the ancient truth displayed in that wonderful Life. Meeting the child-races in Africa or the South Seas, the miracle of a rebirth of their national life has been witnessed again and again, and unsuspected possibilities have been discovered in these simple peoples. Meeting the ancient civilization of China the same miracles are already being witnessed, and in many a hospital and college a new creation has taken place in individual lives. This I have seen time and again with my own eyes, and thereby I am assured that Christ has a gift for China unspeakably great. Without this gift I do not see how China can weather the storm. Whether she acknowledges the source or not, I believe that she will find that she needs the discovery of a personal God to reinforce her ethical system and to give her a philosophy that can carry her through the time of change. Compared with the great educational and medical work done by the missions, this service is even more significant and far-reaching. Nothing will be so great an aid to China in attempting this new synthesis as a demonstration in life of those terrific principles of purity, gentleness, devotion, forgiveness, that we see in Jesus of Nazareth. Many of China's sages have sought to express in words some of those deeper truths that were embodied in that wonderful life. To read the writings of Meh Tzi on Universal Love is to be transported into the atmosphere of the Gospels. Again and again he argues that this principle is good not only in theory, but also in practice. Mencius, in one of his most telling passages, writes: "Love conquers that which is not love, just as water subdues fire. Those, however, who now-a-days practise love, do it as if with one cupful of water they could extinguish a whole wagon-load of burning fuel. This conduct, moreover, greatly encourages those who are not loving—its end is ruin!" Confucius writes: "They sought love and found it; what had they to rue? Is love so far a thing? I yearn for love. Love is here. A man's strength is sufficient for the practise of love, but the people do not try. Should there possibly be any case in which one's strength is insufficient I have not seen it. . . . Could we conquer the lower self and turn to what is right for one day, all mankind would turn to love."

What has the Christian to add to such exalted sentiments? I conceive that he has this to say: "We have record of a life that was actually lived in this spirit, and this life reveals to us the meaning of the whole universe. Its power continues still. We bring you news of that which fulfils the loftiest dreams of your sages." If this be true, the West can bring to China what, as she receives it in her own way, will help her beyond anything else to achieve the deepest purpose of her own inner striving. She will not be turned from her *Tao* or inner nature, she will be given the power to fulfil it in a new and larger way.

5. *The West should stand ready to give her help to China in such ways as China may herself seek for it.* While I believe that harm may be done by thrusting upon China our political or commercial assistance, it seems certain that there will be a number of specific ways in which Chinese will ask for Western help,

CHINA'S GIFT TO THE WORLD 249

and should receive it. Instances of this I have already referred to in the case of political advisers, educational experts, and so forth. A further illustration is that of capital for the development of industries, building railways and so forth. The principle of the International Consortium seems to be a good one, and I think there is a disposition now on the part of foreign capitalists to deal generously with China if she seriously undertakes the task of financial reconstruction. In schools and colleges foreign instructors are sought, and these should be prepared to work under Chinese principals and in accordance with Chinese ideas. In mission undertakings the same is true. These are being increasingly guided by Christian Chinese, and in a number of cases foreigners are now accepting positions under a Chinese committee or individual. It is absurd to suppose that because a man or woman comes from abroad he is therefore competent to control senior workers who are natives of the country. The Chinese leadership in the Y.M.C.A. and Y.W.C.A. is now assured, and a number of the missions are taking steps in the same direction. The Chinese Christians are anxious still to have the help and counsel of foreigners, but they demand a large share of the control, and this demand cannot be set aside. China must judge for herself in what ways the West can best help her.

We have looked at some pages in the long story of China's intercourse with other nations. We have done little more than scan the salient points. As I said at the beginning, I have not attempted a detailed treatment, but have rather sought to give a point of view from which to look more deeply into the problem, and to create an attitude of mind which may help in the formation of right judgments. I recognize that the subjects have been too vast and intricate for adequate handling. I hope, therefore, that I may leave my readers with a taste for more, with a determination, in fact, to become better acquainted with China and with the Chinese, and to use their influence towards creating a juster sense of what China is and may become, and of what we in the West owe to her. Above all I hope that we may have caught some glimpse of the glory that China may become. Drawing from her native wells that penetrating idea of life that is based on maintaining true relationships with all one's fellows, and mingling it with those streams of living water which flow from the Master Personality of our Mediterranean civilization, who can guess what China may yet discover and give to the thirsty peoples of the West ? When Luther and Erasmus were re-discovering the meaning of personal religion and the essentially peaceable character of the Christian Gospel, the Chinese philosopher Wang Yang Ming was promulgating the idea of the investigation of things and showing how by following the intuitive faculty or inner light, man might rise to his true destiny and shake off the shackles of past tradition. The Reformers in Europe found prepared ground, and their doctrines spread like wildfire and sowed the seeds of many a revolution in thought and government. The Chinese philosopher was like a voice crying in the wilderness. But his spiritual heirs are with us to-day. As they proclaim the gospel of personal freedom and universal peace, they find many ready to hear and receive. The new China is arising before our eyes. We of the West hold this terrible power that by our misguided policies, by our materialism and self-seeking, even by our indifference, we may distort this movement of life, and instead of our finding the young hero arising in his strength to join in the onslaught upon ignorance and crime and disease, we may see, through

CHINA'S GIFT TO THE WORLD

our acts, a monster turning his new-found strength against us and all that we stand for. Even to think of such a possibility is almost an outrage on China. But knowing what we have done in the hundred years that are just behind us we have no right to assume that we shall not create the Yellow Peril we talk about. Apart from our action there is and can be no such thing. Rather let China be welcomed into the family of nations; let us show her that we want her, and that we are prepared to treat her as a member of the family; let us give her justice and friendship, respect and sympathy, and the Yellow Peril will be transmuted into the Golden Dawn. China will come as a chief partner in turning into a reality her own dream of more than two thousand years ago: "Under Heaven there is but one Family."

BIBLIOGRAPHY

In the following suggestions for further reading no attempt has been made to give a complete bibliography. Books are chosen mainly with a view to the "general reader." The student will have access to fuller bibliographies.

FURTHER READING ON CHAPTER I

Chinese Characteristics, by Arthur H. Smith. (Oliphants.)

Books of Travel in China which give a sympathetic picture of Chinese life and character, such as *The Yangtse Valley and Beyond*, by Mrs. Bishop, etc., etc.

Village and Town Life in China, by Y. K. Leong and L. K. Tao. (George Allen & Unwin, Ltd.)

Men and Manners in Modern China, by J. MacGowan. (Unwin.)

FURTHER READING ON CHAPTER II

Religion in China, by J. Edkins. (Kegan Paul.) [Chapter II for account of Ancient Sacrifices on Altar of Heaven.]

Village Life in China, by A. H. Smith. (Oliphants.)

Chinese Proverbs, by A. H. Smith. (Kegan Paul.)

The Confucian Classics, Translations by J. Legge. (Kegan Paul.)

An Introduction to the History of Chinese Pictorial Art, by H. A. Giles. (Quaritch.)

A History of Chinese Literature, by H. A. Giles. (Heinemann.)
The Original Religion of the Chinese, by John Ross. (Oliphants.)

254 CHINA IN THE FAMILY OF NATIONS

FURTHER READING ON CHAPTER III

Outlines of Chinese History, by Li Ung Bing. (Commercial Press, Shanghai.)

A Sketch of Chinese History, by F. L. Hawks-Pott. (Kelly & Walsh, Shanghai.)

Annals of the Court of Peking, by E. Backhouse and J. O. P. Bland. (Heinemann.)

The Nestorian Monument in China, by P. Y. Saeki. (S.P.C.K.)

China Year Book 1921–2 (Chapter XII).

Studies in Chinese Religion, by E. H. Parker. (Chapman & Hall.)

China, Her History, Diplomacy and Commerce, by E. H. Parker. (Murray.)

FURTHER READING ON CHAPTER IV

The Foreign Relations of China, by M. J. Bau. (Nisbet.)

China Under the Empress-Dowager, by J. O. P. Bland and E. Backhouse. (Heinemann.)

China, Her History, Diplomacy and Commerce, by E. H. Parker. (Murray.)

FURTHER READING ON CHAPTER V

Modern China: A Political Study, by S. G. Cheng. (Oxford University Press.)

China Year Book 1921–2 (Chapter XXX).

Recent Events and Present Policies in China, by J. O. P. Bland. (Heinemann.)

China Awakened, by M. T. Z. Tyau. (Macmillan.)

FURTHER READING ON CHAPTERS VI AND VII

Korea's Fight for Freedom, by F. A. McKenzie. (Simpkin, Marshall.)

BIBLIOGRAPHY

The Case of Korea, by Henry Chung. (George Allen & Unwin, Ltd.)

Peking, a Social Survey, by Sidney D. Gamble. (Milford.) 21/-.

The Foreign Relations of China, by M. J. Bau. (Nisbet.) 18/-.

Democracy and the Eastern Question, by T. F. Millard. (George Allen & Unwin, Ltd.)

China, Captive or Free, by Gilbert Reid. (George Allen & Unwin, Ltd.)

Modern China : A Political Study (Chap. IX), by S. G. Cheng. (Oxford University Press.)

The Invention of a New Religion, by Basil Hall Chamberlain. (Watts & Co.)

The Far Eastern Question in its Geographical Setting, by Percy M. Roxby. (The Geographical Association, Marine Terrace, Aberystwyth.)

The Imperial Drug Trade, by Joshua Rowntree. (Methuen.)

The War Against Opium. (International Anti-Opium Association, Peking, and Marshall Bros., London.)

FURTHER READING ON CHAPTER VIII

The International Development of China, by Sun Yat Sen. (Commercial Press, China.)

The Christian Occupation of China, Part I, pp. 20–27.

The China Year Book 1921–2 (Chapters IX, X, XVII and XXV).

China Awakened, by M. T. Z. Tyau (Chapters XI, XII and XIII). (Student Christian Movement.)

Village and Town Life in China, by Leong and Tao. (George Allen & Unwin, Ltd.)

The Guilds of China, by H. B. Morse. (Out of print.) (Longmans.)

FURTHER READING ON CHAPTER X

China Awakened, by M. T. Z. Tyau. (Student Christian Movement.)

China To-day Through Chinese Eyes, by various Chinese authors. (Student Christian Movement.) 2/6.

The Problem of China, by Bertrand Russell. (George Allen & Unwin, Ltd.) 7/6.

The Student World (Magazine) 1922. Article by Dr. de Vargas. (Student Christian Movement.)

INDEX

Africa, 247
Agriculture, 176, 180, 187, 239
Altar of Heaven, 33-4
America. *See* United States
   Central America, 230
Amoy, 49, 51, 59
Amritsar, 104
Analects, The, 28, 198, 214
Ancestor worship, 43
Anglo-Japanese Alliance, 108, 134, 163, 165
Anthrax, 187
Anti-Christian Society, The, 222
Antimony, 181
An Fu party, 87
Arab traders, 45
Architecture, Chinese, 27
Arkwright, Richard, 49
Art, Chinese, 24 *et seq.*, 197, 216-17
Australia, 17, 135, 136

Backhouse and Bland, *Annals of the Court of Peking*, 53
Bau, M. J., *The Foreign Relations of China*, 134, 146, 165
Belgian railway syndicate, 67, 131
Bell, Mr., 51
Bible, The, 30, 206, 221
   Old and New Testaments, 222
   The Gospels, 248
Black Dragon Society, The, 138
Bland and Backhouse, *China Under the Empress-Dowager*, 71-2
Bland, J. O. P., *Recent Events and Present Policies in China*, 59, 127
Blythe, Mr., *Saturday Evening Post*, 113
Bokhara, 42

Bolshevism, 169-70, 190, 211
Book of Changes, The, 233
Borneo, 17
Bourbons, 190
Boxer rising, The, 43, 68, 69, 70-3, 163, 201
Boycotts—
   Anti-Japanese, 117, 149
   Anti-U.S.A., 163
   Economic, 175
Brigands (bandits), 90, 106, 129, 179, 236, 240
Buddhism—
   Beginnings of, 41
   Buddhist pantheon, 34
   Influence on China, 54, 231
   Northern form in China, 43
   Persecution, 43
   Success of, 43
   Translations of writings, 42
Burmah, N. and S., 64

Cabinet, the, 95, 159
Canada, 17, 135
Canton, 45, 46, 51, 59, 88, 90-1, 93
Cattle and sheep breeding, 187
Chamberlain, Basil Hall, *The Invention of a New Religion*, 101
Chambers of Commerce, 80, 159, 235
Chang Chih Tung, 65, 68
Chang Po Ling, Dr., 159
Chefoo, 48
Ch'en Ch'ung Ming, 92-3
Cheng, S. G.—
   Modern China, 80, 85
   Opinions quoted, 89
Chengtu, 168, 205
Ch'ien Lung, 50, 65, 69
Ch'ien Yuan Tung, 221-2

258 CHINA IN THE FAMILY OF NATIONS

China—
  Ancient civilization, 37, 197, 231
  Beginnings of foreign influence, 41
  Beset by foreign Powers, 227
  Civil authority should be freed from military domination, 96, 229, 235
  Colonization, 18, 88
  Condition cause of anxiety to world, 99, 137, 195, 211, 225
  Culture, 23
  Driven to militarism, 131, 229
  Early currency, 47
  Economic relations with West—
    Advantages possessed by foreign capitalists, 189
    Competition in trade, 151, 164
    Financial penetration, 118 et seq.
    Forced open by sword, 56
    Trade not wanted, 57, 121, 143
    Trade relations, 54–5
  Emigration, 17, 187
  Exports—
    Tea, silk, oil, oilcake, oil seeds, skins, furs, 149
  Foreign approach always self-seeking, 64, 151, 242
  Foreign intervention, 97, 243
  Genius of, 33, 190
  Gift to the world, 234, 243, 250
  Imports—
    Opium, tobacco, cotton goods, machinery, hardware, iron goods, 149
    Machinery, dyes, drugs, 150
  Influence of Greece and Rome, 44, 219
  Internal mental and spiritual changes, 197
  Internal political changes, 79
  Internal social changes, 187
  International questions faced, 161

China (continued)—
  International relations threatened, 152
  Loans to China, 84, 123
    To responsible Government only, 130, 154, 191
    How money was spent, 160
    Security for interest on loans, 120
    Still requires financial help, 97, 145
  Local self-government, 79
  Looking to West for help, 210, 248
  Manufactures—
    Silk, oilcake, etc., 149
    Yarn, 151, 185
    China, 177
    Various, 183
  Military council, 95
  Military dictatorship, 86–7
  Military relations with West, 56, 62, 143. See Wars
  Navy reorganized under British guidance, 64
  Need of modern army and navy, 210
  North and South, 87 et seq.
    Crisis between, 113
    Northern party, 87, 88, 159
    Southern party, 85, 88, 90–1, 159, 234
    Union of, 83
  Origin of name, 41
  Outstanding needs of China—
    A well thought-out industrial system, 238
    Better system of communications, 239
    Higher moral standards in her public men, 237
    Improved educational system, 240
    Reorganized judicial system, 241
    Strong constitutional government, 234
  Outstanding qualities of nation—
    Adaptability, 22, 195, 239
    Capability, 150

INDEX

China (*continued*)—
 Outstanding qualities of nation (*continued*)—
  Conservatism, 62, 201, 209
  Contentment, 178, 232
  Endurance, 22
  Fairmindedness, 50
  Good sense, 195, 239
  Honesty and integrity in business, 19, 193, 237
  Industry, 22
  Patience, 20, 144, 189, 195, 214
  Peaceableness, 22, 40, 54, 166, 189, 195, 214, 229
  Reasonableness, 21
  Resourcefulness, 22
  Reverence for learning, 22, 201-2
  Shrewdness, 147
  Social sense, 214-15
  Tolerance, 54, 155
 Own internal weakness cause of trouble, 67, 73, 90, 99, 143, 210, 236-7
 Pitfalls of materialism and militarism, 160
 Population, 16-7, 176, 187
 Possessions ceded to Foreign Powers, 59, 64
 Relations with—
  Portugal, 49
  Spain, 49
  Holland, 49
  Russia, 50
  England, 52
  France, 61
  Japan, 100 *et seq.*
 Religious and cultural aspects of relations with the West, 56
 System of selecting officials, 79, 202-3
 Victim of jealous Foreign Powers, 97
 West should give China—
  Time to work out her own salvation, 243
  A more sympathetic understanding, 244

China (*continued*)—
 West should give China (*continued*)—
  Absolute fair play, 245
  A chance to see the best of the West, 246
  Help as China herself asks for it, 248
China Year Book, 183
Chinese Recorder, 222
Ch'in and Ch'u, 39
Ch'ing-teh-chen, 177
Ch'in Shih Hwangti, 40, 41, 47
Christianity, introduction of, 45
Christian Occupation of China, The, 168, 188
Chu Hsi, 198
Chüin Tsï, 214
Chung King, 179
Church, the Christian, in China, 158, 160, 161-2, 223, 238
Cinemas, 244-5
Class war, the—
 Causes of, 193
 Dangers of, 171
 How to avoid, 189
 Road to emancipation, 195
Clemenceau, M., 144
Cochin China, 44, 64
Columbia University, 209
Columbus, 84
Commentaries, 198
Commercial Press, the, 194
Concessions, 119, 146, 242
Confucius, 27, 28, 38, 41, 202, 248
Consortium, 122-3, 144, 153-4, 167, 191, 228, 249
Constitution, the—
 Provisional constitution, 94-5
 Adoption of urgently needed, 98-9
 Constitutional government, 234
Consular jurisdiction, 146
Cornell University, 209
"Correct Meaning, The," 198
Council of Five, 147

Damocles, 111
Denationalization, 227-9

Denmark, 158
Dishonest officials, 64, 83, 87, 96, 210, 214, 228, 235, 237
Disintegration, 227–8
Donald, W. H., 113
Dutch help asked for, 51
Dynasties—
　Ch'in, 40, 79
　Chou, 38, 40
　Han, 42
　Manchu, 19–20, 50, 54, 60, 65, 82, 86, 95, 143, 190, 197–8, 211, 227
　Ming, 48, 49, 50, 198
　Mongol, 47
　Table of, 36
　T'ang, 30, 45, 46, 48
　Tang and Sung, 24, 198

East India Company, 51
Economic imperialism, 118
Education—
　Adult education, 97–8
　Education for citizenship, 97
　Modern education, 68
　Missionary education. *See* Missions
　Public lectures, 205, 217, 246. *See* Student body
Educational associations, 80, 159, 204, 205, 235
Elder Statesmen (Genro), 100, 139
Emperor worship, 101, 125, 137
Emperors—
　Ch'ien Lung, 50
　Ch'in Shih Hwangti, 40, 41, 47
　Hsiang Hsu, 38–9
　Hsieh Ho, 24
　Hsüan Tang, 81, 83
　Hsü Fu, 48
　K'ang Hsi, 50, 51
　Kuang Hsü, 68, 69, 70, 71, 72, 81, 201
　Kublai Khan, 47, 48, 88, 232
　Ming Ti, 42
　Ta Chin, 44
　Tai Tsung, 45
　Wang An Shih, 46
　Wan Li, 50
　Wu Ti, 42
　Yao and Shun, 37, 68

Empress-Dowager (Tsü Hsi), 66, 67, 69, 71, 72, 81, 83, 201
Empress-Dowager (Lung Yü), 83
England. *See* Great Britain
Envoys, foreign, captured and tortured, 61
Erasmus, 250
Exclusion policy, 135, 163
Experiments, 182, 184, 193–4, 205, 239
Extra-territoriality, 119, 144, 145, 146, 169, 241–2

Face-saving, 83, 94, 108
Factories, 149, 150–1, 171, 183 *et seq.*, 192–3, 216
Factory laws, 184, 185, 192
Family life, 31–2
Family system, 79–80, 172–3, 176, 178, 188, 192–3, 202, 212–13, 218
Farquhar, J. N., *Modern Religious Movements in India*, 223
Federated parliament, 236
Federated provinces, 234
Fêng Kuo Chang, 86
Feudal system, 40
Fiume, 131
"Five Relations," 33
Foochow, 59
Foreign controlled services, 87, 120, 166, 246
　Customs, 121, 166
　Diplomatic service, 244
　Post Office, the, 121, 179, 204
　Salt Gabelle, the, 121, 176, 177–8
Formosa, 49, 64, 74, 129, 135, 136, 179
Four Power Pact, the, 145
France—
　War with China, 64
　Gains political and commercial advantages, 66
　Receives Port of Kuang-Chow-Wan, 67
　Sphere of influence, Southern provinces, 67
　China's attitude to France, 167–8

INDEX

France (*continued*)—
  Chinese labourers in France, 210
Fukien, 48, 67, 129, 135

Gambling, 242
Gandhi, 32, 179
Gê Ming, 233
Geneva, 40
Genro. *See* Elder Statesmen
George III, 52-3
George, D. Lloyd, 144
Germany, 66, 108-9, 111 *et seq.*, 138, 147, 158, 168-9
  Youth Movement, 213
Golden Age, the, 37
Golden Dawn, the, 250
Gordon, General, 60
Government Higher National College, 217
Graft, 93, 96, 98, 237. *See* Dishonest officials
Great Britain, 57, 58, 61, 66, 67, 82, 101, 114, 119, 127, 131-2, 134, 136, 151, 154, 164, 165 *et seq.*, 169, 181, 228
Great Learning, the, 30, 173
Great Wall, the, 40-1, 73
Great War, the, 103, 108, 111, 138, 146, 168, 210
Guilds, 32, 80, 174-5, 178, 188, 192, 193, 236

Hankow, 67, 82, 150, 168, 180
Hanyehping Iron Company, 109, 182
Hara, Premier, 139
Harrison, Miss Agatha, 186
Hart, Sir Robert, 166, 246
Hayashi, Count, 134
Hay, Mr. John, 121
Hobson, J. A., *Life of Cobden*, 127
Hodgkin, H. T., *The Christian Revolution*, 184
Home industries, 171, 176, 178, 239
Hong Kong, 91
Hospitals, 156, 168, 246
Hsiang Hsu, 38-9
Hsiang-nu, 41, 42

Hsieh Ho, 24
Hsü Ching Ch'eng, 72
Hsü Fu, 48
Hsü Shih Ch'ang, 86
Hubbard, *The Fate of Empires*, 232
Hupeh, 176
Hu Shih, Dr., 209
Hwei-kuan, 174

Imperial edicts, 68, 83, 201
Indemnities—
  Boxer indemnity, 71, 163, 165, 168
  Opium indemnity, 59
  Taiping indemnity, 61
Industrial self-government, 193, 229, 239
India—
  Mission sent to India, 42
  Indian monks' influence, 43
  Indian ideas influence China, 43-4
  Knowledge of Indian affairs, 92
  Indo-Chinese opium traffic, 127, 166
  India and Korea compared, 136
  British policy matched, 167
  Difference between China and India, 190
Internationalism, 216
International service, 241
International Development Scheme, 191, 192
International Labour Standard, 161, 192
Ireland, 107, 129
Ishii, Viscount, 108, 115
Islam, 45
Italy, 67, 131

Japan—
  Accepts policy of Open Door, 122, 134
  Aggression of Japan feared and resented, 125, 161, 216
  Army organized by Germany, 64, 101

262 CHINA IN THE FAMILY OF NATIONS

Japan (*continued*)—
  Capable leadership, 65, 100, 139
  Case for Japan, the, 135 *et seq.*
  Champion of East against West, 76
  China's condition menace to, 137
  Colonists, 136
  Demoralization of China by Japan—
    Opium and morphia, 127–8
    Prostitutes, 128
    Protection of wrongdoers, 129
    Secret encouragement of internal strife, 130, 137
  Diet, the, 107
  Early Chinese influence in Japan, 48
  Efforts to substitute civil for military control, 139
  Hailed as deliverer of China, 76–7, 134
  Threw away her chance, 76, 100, 102
  Imperial University, 141
  Japanese hegemony, a, 137
  Japanese imperialism—
    A policy of self-defence, 100–1
    Policy indefensible, 102–3
    Economic imperialism, 118, 125–6, 228
    Imperialist policy, 137
    Trend of industrial development, 195
    Moral revulsion of China, 210
    Extreme nationalism, 229
  Labour Movement, 195
  Meiji Era, 101
  Navy built up by England, 101
  Present position between Japan and China, 134 *et seq.*
  Press closely watched and censored, 141
  Progressive leaders and their policy, 140–1

Japan (*continued*)—
  Reasons for entry into Great War, 108
  Japanese régime in Korea, 103 *et seq.*
  Special envoy sent to United States, 115
  Two Japans, 103, 138
  Westernizing of Japan, the, 101, 229
Jesuits, 50, 51, 61
Jesus Christ, 221, 223–4, 246–7, 250
John's University, St., 158
Jordan, Sir John N., 166

K'ang Hsi, 50, 51
K'ang Yu Wei, 68
Kansu, Moslem influence, 45
Kiaochow, 66
Kobë, 141
Koo, Dr. Wellington, 148
Korea, 46, 48, 49, 64, 65, 73–5, 100, 103 *et seq.*, 134–5, 136
Korean proclamation of Independence, 105
Kowloon, 146
Kuang Chow Wan, 67
Kang Hsü, 68, 69, 70, 71, 72, 81, 201
Kublai Khan, 47, 48, 88, 232
Kuo-ming-tang, 85
Kwang Yin, 43

Labour conditions, 117, 178, 183 *et seq.*
  Good conditions necessary, 193
  How to improve them, 189, 190
Labour organizations, 188, 189
La Jeunesse (Shing Tsin Nien), 212
Language, the Chinese, 27–8, 205 *et seq.*, 209, 232, 240
  Bei Hwa, 207, 209
  Dialects, 208
  Ideographs, 27, 208
  Kuo Yü, 207
  Mandarin, 208

INDEX 263

Language (continued)—
  Phonetic script, 208–9
  Syllabary, 44
  Wênli, 206, 208
Lansing, Mr., 115–16, 131
Lansing-Ishii Agreement, 115
Lao Tze, 29
Leadership—
  Creation of leaders, 98, 158, 160, 164, 200
  Lack of, 65, 96, 193
League of Nations, 128, 131, 144, 147, 245
  The earliest League, 38
Lectures, public, 205, 217, 246
Legge, J., *Confucian Classics*, the, 198
"Li," 21
Liang Chi Ch'ao, 68
Liaotung Peninsula, 74, 75
Li Hung Chang, 65
Literature, 27
  Classics, 28, 30, 198, 202, 206, 214
  History, 31, 201–2
  Novel and drama, 47, 206
  Poetry, 30–1
Literati (scholars), 40, 198, 201–3, 232
Literary revival, 197–8, 199, 204–5, 212, 216
Li Ung Bing, *Outlines of Chinese History*, 53
Lin, Commissioner, 58
Liu Chiu Islands, 64
Li Yuen Hung, 82, 85, 89, 96
Livy, 237
Loans—
  Crisp loan, 123
  Foreign loan, 84
  Japanese loans, 123. See Consortium
London, 233
Luther, Martin, 250

Macao, 49
Macartney, Lord, 52, 57
Machinery, introduction of, 178–9
Mackenzie, *The Wonderful Century*, 199

Madagascar, French action in, 104
Makino, Baron, 144
Manchus. See Dynasties
Manchuria, 51, 65, 67, 74–5, 109, 122, 123, 125, 131, 136, 153, 181, 187
Manhood suffrage, 174
Manila, 49
Maon Se-ho, 198
Marcus Aurelius, 44
Margary, Mr., 63
Massacre by Spaniards, 49
Maxim, Hiram, 49
Mazzini, Guiseppe, 233
Mean, Doctrine of the, 33
Meh Tze, 29, 247
Mencius, 29, 32, 41, 79, 214, 248
Mikado, the, 139
Millard, T. F.—
  Democracy and the Eastern Question, 101
  Saturday Evening Post, 112, 123, 126, 128
  Conversation with, 114
Mines, 181
  Nationalization, 182
  Mining, 180, 181
  Mining rights yielded, 66, 181
  Mineral resources, 180, 181
Ming Ti, 42
Missions—
  Missionaries attacked, 59
  Missionaries killed, 63, 70, 156
  Missionary contacts, 155 *et seq.*
  Missionary education, 98, 156, 158, 164, 199, 213, 223, 247, 249,
  Missionary failure, 156–7, 217, 225, 246
  Missionary movement and its inspiration, 157
  Protestant missionaries, 155–6
  Roman Catholic missionaries, 62, 63, 155, 167
Missionary movement as a factor, the—
  In international understanding, 144, 157
  In encouraging Chinese leadership, 158

264 CHINA IN THE FAMILY OF NATIONS

Missionary movement (*cont.*)—
  In solving industrial problems, 195
  In initiating progressive movements, 199
  In pioneering language reform, 206
  In the discovery of personal values, 213
  In giving our best to China, 246
Modern research methods adopted, 187
Mohammedanism, 45
Mongolia, Eastern Inner, 109, 123, 154, 187
Morphia, 127–8
Morrison, Robert, 199
Morrison, Dr., 113
Moscow, mission to, 51, 115
Motono, Viscount, 112, 126
Moukden, 18

Nankai College, 159
Nanking, 83, 89, 159
Nan Tung Chow, 182
National Christian Conference, the, 158, 160, 223
National University (Peking), 209
Nestorian tablet, 45
New Thought Movement, 198, 201, 206, 209 *et seq.*, 230
New York, 232
Ningpo, 59

Olopun, 45
Open door policy, 121, 122, 134, 153, 163, 166, 167, 228
Opium—
  First opium war, 58–9, 143
  Traffic legalized, 62
  Traffic harmful, 119
  Britain puts an end to her trade in opium, 127
  Japan carries on, 127
  Amount imported, 149
  Cause of ill feeling, 165–6
  A grave evil, 242
  Being dealt with sincerely and thoroughly, 245
  Worst side of West shown, 246

Orphanages, 156
Osaka, 141
Ownership of land, 176, 188

Palaces sacked and looted—
  Imperial Palace, 71
  Summer Palace, 61
Pao Ting Fu, 96
Parliament, Houses of, 95, 96
Paris, 131, 147
Peace Conference, 112, 113, 114, 115, 116, 130, 147. See *under* Versailles
Peking, 21, 26, 51, 52, 58, 59, 60, 61, 71, 93, 116, 145, 158, 163, 169, 217, 219, 234
Peking, Social Survey of, 128
Persia, 46
Pescadores, the, 64, 74
Peter the Great, 51
Philip of Spain, 48
Philippine Islands, 17. 49, 67
Philosophy, Chinese, 28, 30, 48, 196, 201, 208, 211, 214
Port Arthur, 66, 74, 131, 146
Presidents of Chinese Republic—
  List of, 78
  Powers of, 95
Press, the, 204
Prime Minister, 86, 89
Profit-sharing, 177. 192, 194
Prostitution, 128, 161
Protestant Christians, 159–60
Proverbs, Chinese, 173, 251
Provincial Assemblies, 81, 85, 234
Provincial autonomy, 97
Provincial self-government, 99, 234, 236

Queen Elizabeth—
  Letter to, 52
  Elizabethan writers, 207

Race prejudice, 164
Railways in China—
  Chinese Eastern Railway, 75
  Peking to Hankow, 67
  Proposed line to Szechuan, 83
  Shantung railway, 159
  South Manchurian Railway, 159

INDEX

Railways in China (*continued*)—
  Trans-Siberian Railway, 74
  Woosung Railway, 179
Railways—
  More needed, 180, 239
  Rights yielded, 66
  Rights refused, 67
  State ownership, 180
Reafforestation—
  In Korea, 106
  Needs attention in China, 187
Reform movements—
  Reforms in education, government and army proposed, 68
  Reforms promoted, 69
  Reforms cancelled, 69
  Stimulus renewed, 76
  Promoted by small minority, 204
Regent, the (Prince Ch'un), 81
Re-integration, 227–30
Religion of China—
  Monotheistic, 34
  Negative in regard to spiritual realities, 43
  No belief in a personal God, 213
  Tendency to substitute æsthetics, 216
  Ethical teaching discounted, 241
  Needs discovery of personal God, 247.
  See also Buddhism, Christianity, Mohammedanism
Religious persecution, 43, 63, 70
Renaissance, the, comparison of European and Chinese, 219 *et seq.*
Republic, the Chinese, 38, 70, 71, 80, 82–3, 84, 90, 125, 144, 190, 200, 210, 237
Revolution, the Chinese, 82, 85, 90, 199, 232, 250
Richard, Dr. Timothy, 199
Roads, 239
Rockhill, Minister, 21
Roman Catholic missionaries, 62, 63, 155, 167
Romanoffs, 190
Rowntree, Joshua, *The Imperial Drug Trade*, 127

Russell, Bertrand, *The Problem of China*, 53, 222
Russia—
  Opens relations with China, 50
  Trouble between the two countries, 51
  Gains commercial and political advantages, 66
  Takes possession of Manchuria, 67
  Demands and gets Port Arthur, 66
  Search for ice-free port, 73
  Permission to build railway, 74
  A dangerous neighbour to Japan, 103
  Opposed to open door policy, 121
  Ousted in Manchuria by Japan, 122
  Imperialist Russia, 167
  Reasons for dislike of Russia, 169–70
Russo-Japanese War, 65, 68, 73, 75–7, 81, 101

Saghalien, 75
Saito, Baron, 106–7
Seattle, 180
Secret ballot, 85
Secret societies, 70
Seiyukai party, 139
Senate, the, 159
Seum King, 41
Shanghai, 59, 150, 182, 186
Shantung, 66, 103, 108 *et seq.*, 131, 135, 144, 147, 168, 207
Shensi, 180
Silver, 57–8
Singapore, 18
Slavery, 161
Small industries, 176–7
Smith, Dr. Arthur H., 20–1
  Village Life in China, 31
Social problems, 160–1, 216
Social revolution, 191
Social service, 215, 216
Social system. *See* Family, the
Social theory, 32
Son of Heaven, 34
South Seas, 247

Soviet, the, 112, 169, 190
Spheres of influence, 66–7, 68, 125, 146, 153–4, 228
State socialism, 46–7, 191, 238
Steamer services, 179
Story-teller, the, 205
Straits Settlements, 17, 136
Strikes, 91, 190
  In Japan, 91, 195
  Student strike, 91, 217
Student body, the—
  Believe they have something to gain from West, 244
  Bolshevism approved by, 190
  Driving force of students, 209
  Ensures democracy, 203
  Foremost in awakening of China, 228
  Graduates of Christian institutions, 98, 158–9
  Graduates of foreign universities, 113, 164
  Graduates of military academy, 131
  Students in United States, 164, 200
  Students in France, 168
  Students in Western schools, 210
  Leaders of New Thought, 211
  Need of dynamic, 217
Sumatra, 17
Sun Yat Sen, 82, 90 *et seq.*, 236
  The International Development of China, 188–9, 191–2
Superstition, 180, 216, 221
Sutras, Indian, 43
Szechuan, 21, 82, 178

Ta Chin, 44
Taiping rebellion, 60–1, 89, 120
T'ai T'sung, 45, 48
Taj Mahal, 26
T'ang Shao Yi, 200
Tao, the, 44, 188, 248
Tao, L. K., *Village and Town Life in China*, 173
Tariffs—
  Demand for fixed tariff, 119
  Tariff reform refused, 133

Tariffs (*continued*)—
  Restrictions in regard to, 146
  Demand for tariff autonomy, 152–3
Tartars, 47
Taylor, Professor, 188
Telegraph system, 179
Theodosius, 44
Three Kingdoms, the, 88
Tientsin, 57, 61, 63, 159, 168
Ting, Mr., *Geological Survey of China*, 181
Tobacco, 149, 153
Tokyo, 107, 115, 134
Tolstoi, Count Leo, 221
Toynbee, Arnold, *The Western Question in Greece and Turkey*, 226–7, 228–9
Treaties—
  With Russia, 51
  Nanking, 59
  With England, 62
  With France, 62
  With Allies, 71
  With Japan, 74
  Between Japan and Russia, 75
  Peace Treaty of Versailles, 106
  China refuses to sign it, 147
  Treaties forced on China, 143, 152
  With Austria, 148
  New treaties with Germany, 168
Treaty ports—
  All ports opened to trade, 51
  All ports closed again, 51
  Five treaty ports opened, 59
  More opened, 62
  Ports as trading centres, 119
  Can they be given up ? 145, 178, 242
Tsushima, Straits of, 75, 77
Tuan Chi Jui, 86–7, 89
Turkey, 228
Twenty-one demands, the, 103, 108 *et seq.*
  Group V, 133
Tyau, M. T. Z., *China Awakened*, 144, 147, 182, 190
Tzi Liu Chin, 177

INDEX

Unconscious influence of West on East, 226-7
Unified National Policy, 235-6
United States, the (U.S.A.), 17, 21, 66, 67, 77, 102, 108, 111, 112, 113, 114-15, 116, 131-2, 135, 143, 150-1, 153, 158, 163-5, 167, 169, 181, 200, 228, 244, 246
United States of China, 93
Unity, 157, 167

Valerius, Publius, 237
Valuta, the, 168-9
Vargas, Dr. Phillippe de, 219
Versailles, 106, 116, 130, 131, 132, 159, 163, 168, 207, 210. *See also under* Peace Conference
Viceroys, 72

Wages, table of Shanghai factory, 185
Wang An Shih, 46
Wang, Dr. C. T., 159
Wang Yang Ming, 250
Wan Li, 50
Wars—
  First war with Britain, 57, 143
  Second war with Britain, 58, 61
  War with Russia, 51
  War with France, 64
  War with Japan, 65, 68, 74
  War with Allied troops, 70
  Great War, 103, 111 *et seq.*, 113-14, 210. *See* Russo-Japanese War
War lords (Military chiefs), 87, 90, 95, 96, 115, 204, 218, 229, 235, 236
Washington, 110, 115, 132, 133, 142, 145, 153, 159, 163, 235, 245

Waterloo, 131
Watt, James, 49
Weale, Putnam, 111
  Fight for the Republic of China, 138
Wei basin, 180
Wei Hai Wei, 66
Wells, H. G., *Outline of History*, 232
Wells Williams, 46
Wen, Dr. S. T., 159
Wén Yu Huei (Literary Society), 219
Wilson, Woodrow, 105, 114, 131, 144
Women's Movement, the, 218
Workers' Educational Association, 98
Wuchang, 82
Wu Pei Fu, 96
Wu Ti, 42
Wu T'ing Fang, Dr., 90
Wycliffe, John, 206-7

Xavier, Francis, 201

Yangtse River, 150, 179
Yangtse Valley, 67, 82, 135
Yao and Shun, 37, 68
Yellow Peril, 251
Yellow River, 38
Yellow Sea, 48
Yen, Dr. W. W., 158
Y.M.C.A., 159, 164, 194, 248
Y.W.C.A., 164, 248
Yuan Shih Kai, 69, 70, 80, 81, 82-3, 84-5, 94-5
Yuan Ch'ang, 72
Yüch Ti, 42
Yui, Dr. David, 159
Yünnan, 67